Your Boss and You

Dale S. Murray

Table of Contents

Foreword

Before I discuss the purpose of this book, I think that it would be good to establish what this book is *not*. If you are looking for a book on being a good leader, this probably is not the book for you. There are plenty of others that provide more in-depth learning. This book is also not intended to help you to manipulate your boss to allow you to do what you want. If you are not interested in developing a deeper working relationship with your boss and putting in the hard work that accompanies that task, then this book is not for you. There are no quick fixes here. Some of the methods that I have laid out have taken months to complete—certainly not days. This book focuses on helping you create a win-win symbiotic relationship with your boss for the betterment of you, your boss, and your organization.

The purpose of this book is two-fold. First, we will examine how to "diagnose" your boss to determine his strengths and weaknesses so that you can adequately develop an excellent working relationship. If he is capable of being someone that you can work with, we will look at how to build that working relationship. However, there are some bosses that you can't work with, no matter how hard you try. In those cases it is best to cut your losses and get out. Therefore secondly, we'll examine how to identify which "bucket" he falls in. Hopefully, you can avoid the needless wasted time and effort of working with a boss who is not interested in you and only focuses on his own self-serving goals.

At points during my career I have found, as have many of us, that I stayed with a bad boss too long. I laid awake many nights, trying to strategize how to work with this person. I rationalized it by telling myself that in the end, there would be rewards for good and hard work. I put in all this effort only to find out that wasn't bearing fruit because I was not meeting expectations that this boss wouldn't or couldn't share with me. In one instance, just after I'd had enough and resigned with a bad boss, I received a phone call from a former co-worker who had left the organization a few months earlier. His departure was in large part due to frustrations with the same boss. During this call he made a comment that hit me right between the eyes: "you never had a chance, he never gave you the leeway to do your job." He was right, as I was never trusted and never able to successfully meet the boss's ever-changing, and sometimes conflicting expectations. I tried to adapt to the changes and develop trust. However, like the Greek mythological figure, Sisyphus, every time I thought I had rolled my rock to the top of the hill it rolled right back down.

If I had known, years earlier, what I knew then, I could have possibly saved myself a lot of sleepless nights trying to figure out how to work with this person. If I had left this boss earlier, I could have gotten back on track and had a fulfilling career instead of suffering with frustration and stagnation. The critical question that I began to center on is, how do I identify that decision point? Should I work with this boss, and if so, how? Or, should I realize that it is not possible and get out from under him? Perhaps through this book, you can think differently about how to work more effectively with your boss so that you can have a more fulfilling career. Or, if you decide to leave your boss, you can do so knowing that you have tried everything that you could have to make it better and leave quickly in order to avoid wasting time in your career.

To accomplish the above purposes, I've divided this book into four parts. In Part One, I will discuss what a good boss is and the importance of taking charge of your career and looking for an opportunity to work for this person. In Part Two, I will discuss those bosses that you should consider avoiding. If you work for one of them, you should strongly consider getting out as soon as you can. In Part Three, I will discuss how to work with those bosses who are neither good nor bad. They are human beings who, like all of us, are flawed. We'll discuss how to identify these flaws and how to work with them to develop a collaborative working relationship. I've labeled Parts One through Three the Good, the Bad, and the Ugly. In Part Four, we'll change gears and discuss how to create more good bosses and fewer bad ones. We'll do this by looking at what organizations can do as well as what you individually can do.

This book is ideally suited for the recent graduate, who has had little experience in the world of work and may not be too sure what he wants to do in his life. I wish that I had this book when I started my career as I might have made some different choices about the bosses that employed me. This will also be an excellent resource book when you are working with a new boss, and you can turn to the appropriate chapter to help you to form a good working relationship with him.

During my career, I've had many bosses, both men and women. I have never found, nor am I aware of any research that indicates that women make better bosses than men or vice versa. I've had good male bosses and bad ones. The same can be said for my woman bosses as well. Since I want to protect the anonymity of the bosses that I've worked for and for the ease of reading, I will always refer to a boss using the male pronoun. I can assure you that in many cases, when using this pronoun, in relationship to a good or bad boss, you can substitute "her" or "she." I have also decided to use the term "team member" when describing the employees, subordinates, or associates that report to a given boss. I used the term organization to refer to an entity that produces a good or provides a service in the public or private sector. I also will use the term "leader" to describe a manager, supervisor, or foreman, since there are so many terms used by different organizations. I will use the term senior leader to describe a boss who is in a policymaking position. They may lead a multi-function business unit or be responsible for delivering a good or service that the organization produces, for example. Please don't infer by this that I mean the quality of leadership; the term refers to the position only.

It is my fervent hope that after reading this book you will be proactive in finding the good bosses to work for, learn to work with the bosses who aren't so good, and quickly leave the bad bosses that will impede your career success. You shouldn't meekly accept the fact that your boss is creating a miserable work life for you. Instead, you now have informed choices and options to do something about it.

Part One

The Good

Chapter One

Your Boss and You

Over the 45 years of my career, in working for someone else, I've worked for a lot of bad bosses and, fortunately, some good ones. Some of these individuals were such abysmal leaders that they couldn't lead a kindergartener down a sliding board during recess, even if the child were sitting at the top ready to go down. Others were friendly individuals that were just in way over their heads. I have worked for incompetent bosses who were placed in a leadership role by an organization that thought the person would do less damage leading others than they would in a technical role. Other bosses were political animals who spent more time focusing on form rather than substance as a way to please senior leaders. I was able to work around the weaknesses of some of these bosses and learned to get things done. With others, it was impossible to be successful. In those cases, I had to get out from under them and their dysfunctional leadership style, because I was losing sleep at night and it was affecting my health. Their dysfunctionality was causing me to question my abilities because I was blaming myself for the problem. It was a type of self-blaming, similar to what you hear from one of the partners in an abusive relationship.

I have also worked for many good bosses, those that created a positive vision of the future for which my team members and I got excited. Others took a stand for the right issues and worked through resistance, even if that resistance was from senior leaders. I worked for good bosses who took over in a crisis and rallied others to the cause of fixing problems, by utilizing the motivation and creativity that others bring to work with them. These bosses helped me to discover skills, motivations, and abilities that I didn't know that I had. This helped me to be successful, not just in working for them but with other bosses in the future.

Because of my career experiences in the HR field, I have had a unique perspective on these individuals. Besides directly working for them, I have had to fire bad bosses that poorly lead other people. Some of these bosses were bad because they worked for a bad boss themselves. They had been great employees until they started working for a bad boss who so poorly led them that they failed. Much of my HR experience centered in the area of Talent Management. Specifically, I helped develop systems and processes to improve the organizations to identify and develop future bosses.

I have coached executives on how to deal with their own bad bosses as well as with how to deal with a subordinate bad boss who worked for them. Many times, an organizational leader would summon me to his office, frustrated by the poor performance and/or ineffectiveness of a subordinate boss. Sometimes these leaders were receiving complaints from team members about the way that this boss was behaving.

I have also coached many employees on how to deal with their bosses. I listened to their anguish as they described a boss who was draining their motivation and in its place, filling the void with cynicism and depression. I helped interview and onboard many of these employees, several of them filled with great ideas, ready to apply their experience for their organization's benefit. In many cases one individual had destroyed all that energy and drive by his belittling micro-management and lack of trust. I've worked with people who were looking forward to a career as a leader, only to see that motivation squashed by a bad boss. "If this is the way that you have to act like a boss in this organization, I want no part of it," is a common refrain.

I've delivered harsh feedback to bad bosses and tried to help them to improve, as well as tried to help the team members who worked for these bad bosses to thrive or at least survive. As an external consultant for other organizations, I assessed candidates for management roles as part of their hiring process in order to facilitate the process of hiring the right bosses. I also gave these organizations feedback on their internal bosses so that they could develop them to be more productive. In the process of delivering this feedback, I noticed something extraordinary about those individuals who we assessed as both good or bad bosses. We asked—independent of the assessment results which were intended to evaluate leadership ability—for senior management to evaluate those who were tested and to rank their overall performance on the job. We compared these performance results to the assessment results and found that those considered as high performers on the job scored high in the assessment for leadership skills; in other words they displayed the characteristics of a good boss. Conversely, those that were low performers scored low in the assessment. Scoring low meant that they possessed the characteristics of a bad boss.

If you've been in the world of work long enough, you've worked for bad bosses. Team members dealing with a bad boss develop coping mechanisms such as "checking out" and just going through the motions or playing the victim and blaming the organization for putting somebody in charge who is incompetent. I know that I did this on many occasions, early in my career. I applied typical coping mechanisms such as waiting him out or focusing my energy on aspects of my life outside of work. This was energy that could have been used to obtain higher levels of performance if I had worked for a boss that actually cared about me reaching those heights by providing obtainable expectations.

The danger of relying on these coping mechanisms can manifest in two ways. Firstly, there is an impact on organizational performance. The Gallup organization has conducted several surveys over the past few years on the subject of employee engagement. Engagement is critical because engaged employees display discretionary effort, the kind of energy that drives exceptional performance, and organizational success. Not surprisingly, Gallup found that employee engagement relates to increased organizational performance as measured by higher customer satisfaction, productivity, and quality, and lower absenteeism and turnover[i].

For team members to be engaged, they need to feel that they are doing something that is valuable and that interests them. They also need to be able to use a variety of their skills. Not surprisingly, the boss has a great deal of impact on this engagement through the way that he provides feedback on performance or provides autonomy as to how the work is performed. In examining all the variables that create employee motivation, Gallup found that it was the boss that impacted engagement the most. In particular, a good boss had the most significant impact on employee engagement. The study further went on to say that only 30% of employees are engaged at work[ii]. To sum this up: a good boss creates engaged employees. Engaged employees mean higher levels of organizational performance. Higher levels of organizational performance mean job security and growth.

The second danger in relying on a coping mechanism when dealing with the boss is the impact on our psyche. By actuating the negative, bad bosses cause us to question our competence. The ways that they *don't* communicate with us or withhold needed feedback cause us to question our abilities when we are passionate about trying to do a good job. Their micromanagement and lack of empowerment squash the drive and energy that is inherent in all of us. Behavior displayed by the bad boss can lower our self-esteem. All too often, damaged self-esteem doesn't rise when we leave work; rather we take that home with us. Issues from work frequently spill over into our personal lives. They affect the lives of our loved ones and cause us health problems.

When you decide that you can no longer work for your current boss, or you want to find a boss that can challenge you more, it's time to make a change. Let's suppose that you don't want to leave the organization that you are working for. In this instance you should begin to look for a good boss to work for as opposed to just looking for the type of work that you want. It would be great if we could find both a great boss and great work, of course. I am suggesting that of the two—a great boss or great work—the great boss should carry more weight. The work itself should meet your qualifications, and you should find it at least mildly interesting. I suggest that this is a realistic and obtainable goal. The reason that I'm weighting the great boss so profoundly over the work is that the great boss can turn work that meets your minimum standards into something exciting. On the flip side, a bad boss can take exciting work and turn it into misery. Why work for a bad boss when you can work for a good one who will engage you in the work that he is doing? We are going to discuss how to work with bosses extensively in the upcoming chapters. However, to help you to feel empowered to take action to change bosses when it is time to do so, I will outline a doable process to help you.

In most organizations, there are stories about the good bosses that tend to float around the water cooler and the cafeteria. Maybe there is a colleague who has a friend who works for your organization who has a good boss. If you have worked in your organization long enough, you could probably name at least a couple of bosses that you've never worked for but have heard others talk about as being good. Before you make a career move and take the risk involved in such a move, you ought to do everything that you can to verify this individual is a good boss.

I suggest that it would be a good idea to sit down with some of the people who work for those bosses and ask them the questions below. In future chapters, you will see why I selected these particular questions. For now, let's say that the answers to these questions get at the heart of being a great boss. In addition to the item to be asked, I have also included a blurb on the intention behind the question. The purpose of this is to provide guidance in asking follow-up questions if you don't get clear enough answers the first time.

Question to Ask	The Intention Behind the Question
Tell me about the feedback that you receive about your performance? When does it happen? How often does it happen?	Good bosses give honest and regular feedback. They freely give the good and the bad news, and they treat them the same. Team members can make improvements because of the helpful feedback.
Tell me about the quality of work that your boss assigns you?	Good bosses trust their subordinates with the critical challenges that the workgroup is facing. These bosses know that you will put your best effort into this type of work.
Tell me about the autonomy that your boss gives you?	Good bosses give free rein in accomplishing assigned work because they know that you will do your best work when you have the freedom to decide how to do it.
Tell me about how your boss utilizes your skills to accomplish critical work?	Good bosses match the needs of the job with their subordinate's skills, knowledge, and abilities to maximize performance.
Tell me how your boss seeks and values your input on the best ways to accomplish the mission of your group?	Good bosses want their people to be involved in important decisions so that they can maximize performance and feel ownership for positive results.
Tell me how your boss deals with resistance to needed changes, even if it comes from more senior management?	Good bosses take a stand to do the right things and defend it from senior management when a more politically motivated leader would fold in the face of resistance.
Tell me about how your boss introduces new changes to your team that are aligned with its mission?	Good bosses embrace needed changes and display courage in bringing them about.

It is important to ask more than one person these questions, because of individual bias. What you are looking for is common answers from different people. I realize that this is quite a time investment, and it may seem intrusive to some of your friends to put them on the spot like this. The effort that I have outlined is essential because I've found that even a bad boss has an individual who works for him that likes the experience. I remember one time talking to a young technical professional who was working for a person who most in the organization considered a bad boss. However, this technician sang the praises of this boss. The boss had requested that this technician come work for him because he possessed a technical skill that this boss wanted. As a result of this, he was highly compensated and received regular promotions. In this case the technician's motivation and abilities fit the niche that the boss was looking for, and since the boss didn't want to spend his time in this technical area, he gave the technician the freedom that he wanted. If you rely only on this technician's feedback, you'll get a very different story about this boss's qualities than the norm.

If instead of finding a new good boss to work for, you've decided to work with your current one, there are a few guiding principles that you need to keep in mind. As a foundation for the tactics I will outline, these guiding principles will be critical to your success in working with your boss. In the upcoming chapters, we will discuss ways to work with a dysfunctional boss with the intent of developing a good working relationship. After presenting each boss, I will outline the tactics to deal with each of them. However, bear in mind that these guiding principles are universal across the board and are valuable in developing and improving upon any boss relationship.

First and foremost, honesty is paramount. Be honest in how you deal with your boss and how you assess your working relationship with him. Breaking this down: being honest means honoring your commitments. It also means seeking feedback and be willing to take it non-defensively. A healthy working relationship also means giving feedback and being transparent about your concerns. It's a two-way street; be honest and expect honesty from others.

Secondly, work for a <u>win-win</u> relationship. Your success is dependent on your boss being successful. Every time that you go to the boss and ask him to make an effort to change the way that he manages you, you need to think about how he will benefit as a result. How will his actions towards you make him more successful in accomplishing his goals?

Thirdly, you need to commit to <u>taking the initiative</u>. Your boss is probably not going to come to you seeking ways to lead you better. If he does this, chances are he is already doing many of the right things. The bosses that we are going to discuss in this book are the ones who probably think that they are doing the right things already. Or, they are afraid of asking this question, because they aren't looking forward to the answers that they will receive. If you are waiting for your boss to come to you about how to lead you better after he attends that leadership development program, know that you have a better chance to hit the lottery. You need to take responsibility for developing a collaborative working relationship.

Fourthly, you need to <u>be resolute</u>. The "quick kills" in improving the working relationship between you and your boss are going to be few and far between. It's a slow and labor-intensive process. Rarely is it linear, as there will most likely be setbacks. Many of these will be outside of you or your boss's control. New senior leadership, organizational changes, and business competition, to name a few, may impact the relationship that you have with your boss. I've seen a good boss suddenly turned into a micromanaging autocrat because his boss placed new expectations on him.

The way that bosses behave doesn't just affect the material things in our life, such as pay and career; they affect our self-esteem and that spills over into our personal lives. They impact how we behave towards the people that we love. We shouldn't blindly submit to the bosses that our organizations assign us to work for and hope for the best. Instead, we should take control of our careers and manage that relationship for the betterment of our organization and ourselves.

Chapter Two

The Good Boss

When I was fifteen, after an undistinguished career of selling greeting cards and flower seeds door to door and running a paper route for the county newspaper in my neighborhood, I decided to enter the world of regular employment where I would receive a paycheck. After all, one could not purchase many rock albums from the commission generated by selling zinnia seeds.

I took a job working at an orchard for $1.35 an hour, a princely sum in 1972. The work was full time during the summer and after school and Saturdays during the school year. My Steppenwolf collection was going to be the envy of the neighborhood with all the money that I would earn. What I didn't anticipate was the work was going to be brutal. As is the case for most 15-year-olds, my work habits had not fully matured.

One day after work, my boss, the orchard's owner, pulled me aside and gave me what later become known to me as the performance discussion. He pointed out specific examples of poor performance and told me that he expected better. The boss ended the conversation talking about all of the challenges that his business was facing and how he needed my help and what responsibilities I would have if my performance improved. He spoke to me about how I could fit into the "big picture." Being able to recall this so many years later is a testament to the impact this discussion had on me. What struck me most about this discussion was that I felt good afterward. I felt like I was important to this boss because he took the time to talk to me about my poor performance and didn't diminish my self-esteem. Even as a 15-year-old, I could tell that this boss cared about me and my success. I wanted to do my best for him and, most importantly, for myself.

The next spring, the orchard adopted a new product line: pick-your-own strawberries. I was assigned a customer service role, which was the role that the boss had suggested for me as part of the big picture that he had outlined the previous summer. I enjoyed this new job; working with customers was something that stimulated my interest. This boss saw something in me the past year that I hadn't noticed myself. He saw that I was good at working with others, that I gravitated to other people. This very well could have been the spark that ignited a career in human resources, years later.

At the end of the season, the boss called me in for another discussion about my performance. The tenor of this discussion was much more positive than the one from the previous summer. He gave me very positive feedback on my customer service abilities. He asked if I would be interested in taking over running one of his road-side sales operations that he was starting, which would be an uptick in responsibility since I would now be on my own running a piece of his business. This increased my confidence in myself and my ability to handle more challenges in the future.

He saw something in me that I didn't and brought it out for both the benefit of his organization and me. How did he do that? He never attended a leadership development program. Since this was the 1970s, there weren't many books on leadership from him to read. He had nothing more than a high school education, so that rules out the executive MBA at a prestigious university. Since this was his own company with no HR department, nobody gave him a policy manual to follow or even a company value statement that he could carry around in his wallet.

What my boss did have was a value system that had, at its core, a belief in the human spirit. People are bright, creative, trustworthy, and inherently want to do great things. He wasn't Pollyannaish—he realized that there was a small percentage of miscreants in this world that shouldn't be trusted. I saw him deal quickly and directly with those individuals. However, his work was guided by his beliefs and these were put into practice in dealing with the teenagers that he had hired over the previous ten years of running his business. He practiced managing people through trial and error, always anchored by that core set of beliefs that guided him on how to obtain the best performance from the people that worked for him.

Working for this boss was indeed a gift. He saw strengths in me and brought them out, a lesson that stuck, years later, as I started thinking about how I could leverage my strengths to become successful. He helped me to improve my work habits and end those practices that were counterproductive. Specifically, I realized that I needed to take my work more seriously. He showed me the power of direct, honest, and positive feedback. What I mean by positive feedback is that even though the message might be challenging to hear, it indicates that if there is an improvement, good things will follow. Most importantly, when leaders honestly care about their subordinates and create high expectations for them, they will be paid back by delivery of exceptional performance.

This boss displayed empathy for those who worked for him. In my career every good boss that I worked for showed empathy, and every bad boss that I worked for did not. It's not so much that these good bosses articulated empathetic feelings; instead, they *acted* with empathy. Empathy gets a bad rap because it tends to be very misunderstood and conflated with its synonym, sympathy. I've personally experienced several senior organizational leaders who have specifically disqualified bosses for promotion because they behaved empathetically. They see it as a sign of weakness and prohibitive to being effective as a boss. Empathy is the fuel that powers the engine that is the good boss. Without empathy, there is no understanding. Understanding a team member enables a boss to know motivations, strengths and weaknesses. Without this knowledge, there can be no empowerment, and without empowerment, there is no superior performance.

Those two words are very different. Sympathy is *feeling* someone's pain; empathy is *understanding* it. You don't need to feel somebody else's pain to realize that they are in it. This empathetic state of mind enables the good boss to connect with all those people around him (his boss, peers, and subordinates). He is interested in what they think and their motivations. This boss strengthens his relationship with others because they feel that they are genuinely understood.

It is in tough times when it pays off for a boss who is known for his empathy. Empathy builds trust and a strong relationship with team members, both of which are essential for working through challenges. In my example, even though I was 15 years old and never heard the word empathy before, I knew that this boss cared about me while he was pointing out my deficiencies. So much of the work of management in these tough competitive times is to drive change, whether that means higher levels of performance or new work responsibilities. The boss who has not connected with his team and not developed a trusting relationship will very often come up short when it comes to obtaining a commitment to change.

Good bosses also seek input from subordinates in making decisions that impact them. Good bosses believe that the people who work for them are bright, imaginative, and capable. They believe that their team members have great ideas and want to share those ideas because they care about the success of their organizations. I once worked for a good boss who brought his team together once per week to discuss the critical goals that we were all responsible for and sought our input on how to accomplish them. These were the same goals that he was held accountable for by his boss, so we knew that they were essential and that our input counted for something; therefore, we wanted to do our best.

As a way to "seed' the creativity of subordinates, good bosses love to share information about the challenges the organization is facing. For example, when I worked for a manufacturing company, the boss would routinely share data about defects, product costs, or safety issues. This information was posted in the work area at a set time each week. It would be reviewed a few days later in a team meeting. As soon as the new information was posted on the work area's bulletin board, people would leave their work stations and hover around it. You could see the "high-fives" when the results were excellent and the instant problem solving when results were less than expected. Good bosses inherently believe that people produce excellent results if only you give them the resources in which to do it. The simple act of providing people with data that they can use, and that is meaningful to them, will automatically cause them to alter their behavior. People typically want to be successful; they don't need to be told to perform when you've already provided them with the target that they need to achieve. People naturally like to win and accomplish their expectations, goals, and objectives. All they need is a clear direction, feedback on those expectations, and space to achieve them.

Another characteristic of a good boss is giving quality feedback. I have been amazed over the years in how organizations invest time and money in teaching their employees how to provide feedback. So much of giving good feedback is a desire to want to be helpful to the feedback recipient. The desire is something that you can't train for—you have to come equipped with it. If you possess that desire, the vast majority of the time, you will be successful. You don't need to teach people how to do it. We've become used to the terms positive (excellent) and negative (corrective) feedback. Very often, we learn to balance these two types of feedback to maintain the esteem of our employees. Good bosses believe that this is ridiculous. All feedback is delivered in such a way as to be helpful; therefore, it is all positive. When good bosses have feedback, they give it unreservedly, letting the chips fall where they may, as in the example that I gave earlier from my personal experience when I was 15 years old. His feedback was firm. If I didn't improve, I would have been fired. One would expect that I would walk away feeling bad. However, I felt good because I could feel, even though I was emotionally immature, as most 15-year-olds are, that he cared about me and my future. I could tell that he wanted me to improve and he believed in me. I didn't want to let him down, because I would be letting myself down in the process.

This boss did something else with this feedback that I've seen other good bosses do. He used it as a platform for a more extensive discussion about my ongoing development. If the feedback is indicating a performance deficiency, there tends to be a discussion about future opportunities that can be unlocked by showing an improvement. For example, after he pointed out my performance deficiencies, he told me what I needed to do to improve. This boss was setting up a new product line, and if I cleaned up my act, I would be part of the team that was going to support it. If I improved, he would make me more of an integral part of his organization and offer more challenges. Good bosses believe that that challenge motivates the people that work for them; their team members want to grow. To this boss, as a result of this feedback, everybody wins: the subordinate, the boss, and, most importantly, the organization.

Good bosses are very much inclined to use "win-win" as a way to resolve a disagreement or gain support for a position that they are taking. In the feedback example that I presented earlier, my boss wanted to gain a better performing employee by changing my behavior. In so doing, it would create career opportunities for me. We both "won" something as a result of my improvement. Good bosses use this philosophy in dealing with everybody around them, including peers and bosses, as the default condition. They aren't idealistic—they understand that not everybody that they collaborate with wants win-win or is capable of achieving it. However, good bosses also realize that they need to maintain a collaborative relationship with others to achieve their goals. Forcing someone else to lose, to obtain a short-term win, will only damage the relationship of those around them who must provide needed support. A little bit of effort in trying to understand the needs of the person with whom they have a conflict and finding a way to meet both parties' needs will pay big dividends.

Another characteristic of a good boss is the inherent way that they display trust, even if at times they get blind-sided by untrustworthy behavior in others. Explicitly, the good boss trusts you to do great work and believes that your autonomy is the best way to accomplish your responsibilities after providing appropriate direction and resources. He fully expects you to put your creativity and initiative into the work. In his mind, you may very well achieve something more significant than he imagined himself as a result. An example of this is the way that the good boss, in my case, gave me the responsibility of managing his roadside sales operation. I was out there by myself, with the cash box, trusted by my boss, even after my previous performance deficiencies.

Good bosses centralize the work that is assigned, to further your spirit of creativity and initiative. By this, I mean that they are empowering you to take on as much of the whole task as possible as opposed to decentralizing it or breaking it down to small chunks. The whole task usually entails managing one of your team's outputs, such as placing someone in charge of lining up the resources, meeting the needs of your customers, and delivering on commitments to the organization. This kind of behavior is the polar opposite of what bad bosses tend to do. They break the work down into as small chunks as possible and limit freedom of movement so that they can monitor and control it more easily.

This strategy is important because those good bosses know that you are going to get excited about the work and see the fruits of your labor much more than if you were responsible for a small discreet piece of the whole task. You will get to see it from beginning to end, and the impact of your hard work will be readily apparent. Your excitement translates into your desire to do your best without having to be directed. My first boss assigning me to run his road-side sales operation was an excellent example of this principle. He left to me to determine what to sell, what to keep in inventory, how to set up my displays and determine the best time to be there to get the best sales.

The bottom line is those good bosses create an environment where subordinates do their best. If you find that you are reaching down inside and producing effective results that you've never achieved before, then you are probably working for the type of good boss that we have been discussing. It is these bosses that make us feel good about who we are and proud of the work that we are doing. We leave our jobs at night feeling fulfilled and that we've added value to our organization and ourselves.

The good boss that I described in this chapter was not highly educated. He never attended a leadership training course or read books chronicling great bosses. What he possessed was a value system that centered on a belief in the power of the human spirit. This boss believed that human beings could do great things if leaders give them the tools and the freedom to use them to achieve great results.

Good Bosses....	Why It Positively Impacts Performance
Provide honest and complete feedback.	Nobody can consistently achieve top performance in a vacuum. They need information about what they are doing well that can be leveraged for success and what they are not doing well so that corrections can be made.
Believe that others are motivated to want to succeed.	The way we naturally behave is based upon our beliefs. Team members normally strive to fulfill the expectations that bosses set for them. If we believe that team members can be successful, then we set high expectations for them. If you desire superior performance, set expectations accordingly.
Display empathy towards others.	By empathizing with team members we achieve an understanding of their strengths, weaknesses and motivations. Therefore, the strengths can be leveraged for further achievement and the weaknesses that could prove an obstacle can mitigated.
Seek others' input on the issues that impact them.	The best way to improve results is to seek the advice of those who are deeply enmeshed in trying to achieve those results. These team members have a unique perspective because of their involvement. Want the best advice on how to prevent a fire in your home? Ask a firefighter.
Share important information relating to organizational success.	By providing information on how team members are doing in achieving their objectives, they give them the opportunity to act on that information without being explicitly directed to do so.
Develop the capacity of	The only way to meet ever changing

team members.	requirements to perform, which all organizations face today, is to continually develop the capacity of those who need to achieve those results.
Inherently trust team members.	When team members are trusted to meet challenging targets and given the freedom to achieve them they naturally work towards success. If they aren't trusted and not provided with the freedom to achieve these results, there will be mediocre performance because they can't deploy their skills and motivation to the fullest.
Give team members the whole task to perform.	If team members are given the whole task with a deliverable result that they can see is significant; then they will be motivated to achieve. If they are provided with a "small chunk" of the whole task, they could lack a connection to its significance and may not see the need to turn in their best performance.

Chapter Three

You Need to Find a Good Boss to Work for

A few years ago, I was supporting a process to help organizational leaders to develop their top talent. I thought that it might be a good idea to speak with a group of these leaders to understand their success formula, which could be replicated to develop rising young talent. I interviewed a group of 20, asking them to reflect on their careers and tell me what events happened or experiences that they encountered that were pivotal in helping them to be as successful as they were. The idea here was to take this list of best practices and turn it over to aspiring leaders so that they could incorporate this into their development.

Many of the answers that I got were not surprising. The list of critical experiences included being placed in charge of fixing something that was broken or starting a new operating unit. Opening an international office or being put in charge of multiple businesses for the first time were also key experiences for many. The interviewees also said that they had exposure to senior leaders and were assigned challenging projects where there was some risk of failure. There was so much risk and exposure in many of these cases that success or failure would have become known to senior leaders, and failure could have had a detrimental effect on their careers. They also said that they were kept in roles long enough so that they could learn from mistakes. They were able to adjust after making mistakes, then to try to new ways until they were successful.

However, two things came out of that study that were surprising. First, each of the individuals pointed to learning from a good boss early in their career. For each of them, this was in their formative years. They had just graduated from the university with technical degrees and started their careers, trying to put their education into practice. Each ended up working for a boss that challenged them, tapped into their motivations, and expanded the base of their skills, knowledge, and abilities. As an example, very early in his career one of the interviewed leaders worked for a boss who frequently gave him significant problems to solve. This boss increased the quality of the experience by asking this future leader to bring him two viable solutions to address every challenge he was assigned. He said that this taught him a valuable lesson; that there is usually more than one way to solve a problem. Moreover, after he stopped working for this boss, he naturally continued looking for multiple solutions to every problem that he encountered. He also expected the same thing from his subordinates.

All of these leaders said that they had terrible bosses at various times, just like the rest of us. However, for them, a great boss early in their career helped them to realize what they were capable of and brought out the best in these future executives. You might say that these great bosses were a catalyst that got these individuals moving in the right direction. Similarly to my first boss, who believed that I would be successful working with customers (something that I hadn't internalized at the time), the bosses of these future executives saw something in them.

The second surprising finding had to do with how each individual came to work for his good boss. They weren't just lucky to have been assigned to work for this person. Instead, they sought them out, even if this meant that they had to leave the current career track that they were in at the time. I was struck by the consistent story that was relayed to me by these executives. They described how they got to quickly know the organization, its processes, products, and bosses. During that educational process, they began to scope out leaders that they wanted to work for who were doing exciting things and had a reputation for being a good boss. These future executives approached this targeted good boss and outlined to him how they could add value to his organization if he agreed to hire them. It's important to note that this organization, like most, didn't encourage this type of free thinking from its professionals. Instead, it had very much a top-down management style when it came to making career decisions for others.

What these good bosses did for these young professionals was transformational. These bosses challenged their team members to new ways of thinking and gave helpful feedback. These individuals were trusted and empowered with high expectations that involved taking risks. The bosses gave them exposure to senior leaders and other parts of the organization. However, the most important factor was that these bosses were role models. When these young professionals entered the ranks of management, they emulated those early good bosses. Those bosses set the standard to follow. Later, when these individuals worked for bad bosses and saw the difference in performance that resulted, the experience helped to cement the way that they determined they would lead others in the future. If these individuals had not had the influence of that inspiring boss early on, they would most likely not have been as successful in their later careers.

I had a similar experience as these executives, early in my career. I identified a great boss that I wanted to work for and made a career move that was probably the most significant in my entire work life. It was the catalyst in focusing me on what I wanted to do with the rest of my career. After leaving my job at the orchard, I finished college and bounced around a couple of dead-end posts trying to survive the recession of the late '70s. I found what I thought was an ideal job for me as a first-level leader in a steel mill. It was exciting, interesting and I enjoyed managing. However, this was a tough time to be in the business as foreign competition was driving down profits. Cost cutting and finding inexpensive ways to boost production and improve quality were the keys to organizational survival. To that end, a senior leader decided to bring a team together from around the organization to elicit their ideas on how to make improvements. He knew that these individuals had great ideas and suggestions, they just needed a forum to express them.

This senior leader did not have a traditional style for that industry, which seemed to be laden with leaders who preferred to declare war on the union to cut costs. Instead, this boss shifted the paradigm and developed a partnership. He also made some leadership changes bringing some new people from other companies who were more successful than ours had been, which in turn challenged the status quo of the current level of leadership's thinking. I also liked the concept of bringing together smart and dedicated people to develop some specific ideas on how to make improvements, present them to senior leaders, and see their recommendations implemented. As a first-level leader, I worked with the individuals who would be involved with this process, and I found they had a tremendous amount of knowledge of the business, great ideas, and a desire for the organization to succeed in these troubled times.

At the start, it was just the senior leader and my boss who met with this team of volunteers, every other Saturday morning. At our next management staff meeting, the department head shared what was coming out of these sessions. I decided to attend the next Saturday's meeting to see and hear the discussion for myself. That meeting was quite an educational experience for me. There were about 20 team members from all over the organization, brainstorming ideas on how to make improvements. Some of the ideas were wild, requiring large amounts of capital far beyond the organization's needs, while others were simple things that could get done right away and have an immediate impact.

I was impressed by the style of the senior leader who was leading the meeting. He was able to keep the discussion positive even when issues came up that could open old wounds between leadership and the union. I knew many of the employees who were part of the group, but I hadn't seen them in this setting before. Some of these individuals hadn't finished high school, but they were suggesting complex solutions that raised the eyebrow of the chief engineer, who was also in attendance. He, too, was impressed by some of the frame-breaking ideas that were brought forward by these team members.

The following week the senior leader, during a walk-through of our department, pulled me aside and asked what I thought about the meeting. I told him that the concept was great and that it was clear that the payoffs for the organization would be significant. The team was comprised of a cross-section of employees from the entire organization with lots of problems and useful ideas on solving them. The problem was that they were unable to focus on specific issues common to them all; therefore, the discussions tended to be high level and, therefore, difficult to address issues like organizational morale. Then, almost reflexively, I told him that I would like to help by taking the responsibility of leading a team. Perhaps I could work with a subset of the larger group and address a much more focused problem that would be relevant to all of the employees in that team. The senior leader liked the idea, and after clearing it with my boss, he put it to the team at their next meeting. Everyone seemed to like the idea, and a sub-group idea was put into practice so that they could address a specific issue that they were all facing.

Beginning next Saturday, I began to work with a sub-team focused on a much more specific project, a new method to improve productivity in one of the organization's subgroups. My role was to facilitate the team through the problem-solving process. This senior leader had faith in me even though he and I both knew that I was doing something that I had never tried before. I didn't want to disappoint him and betray this faith in me nor let myself down; after all, I asked for this assignment. After a few weeks of study, the team presented its findings and recommendations for an improved process, which were promptly approved and implemented. The senior leader was pleased with the output and my contribution to the process.

Following the presentation, he sat down with me and reviewed what had happened and asked me what I thought about my career with this company. I told him that I got a lot out of leading this team personally, as well as having produced value for the organization, and that I would like to work for him in leading this team or other teams like it in the future. He told me what he saw in me while taking on this project and how it brought out my strengths. Finally, he informed me that he was looking at making this quality circle effort a permanent fixture and asked me if I would be willing to lead it full time. The entire organization was to be supported by this initiative. My role would not be to lead a team part-time but to manage a process of establishing teams organization-wide. I jumped at the chance, and my work life was forever changed. Sure, I was interested in the work, that's what caught my eye. However, it was this boss's great leadership that created this process; nothing existed before he gave birth to it. His excellent leadership took that process from concept to reality. He rallied support for it by convincing the naysayers. For the next two years that I worked for this person, I grew more than in any other similar period. That growth came as a result of both working for a good boss and being very early in my career.

It was the impact of two good bosses that helped shape my future. My first boss gave me the essential tools that I would need to be successful in any walk of life and help me to realize that my career would be one where I would work with and through other people. Another boss helped me fine-tune my strengths and to focus. They helped me to understand what was important to me because of the environment that they created. I learned what motivated me, what abilities I had, and what skills I needed to develop. Before this most recent boss example, my career was rudderless. Now, I had a sense of direction. I still had much work to do before I would have a better understanding of how to be successful and avoid failure. However, I now had a foundation on which to base this future success.

Identifying a good boss to work for early in your career is critical. A good boss will give you the opportunity to tackle challenges that will hone your strengths and motivations, as we saw in the study I did of organizational leaders. However, I've worked for good bosses at every stage of my career and grown as a result, no matter how far along I was. Finally, you can't depend upon luck and hope that your organization will assign you to work under a good boss. You need to take responsibility and display the initiative to find one for yourself. Your organization probably won't support your efforts to find a good boss. However, I've never known anybody who was punished for taking action like this to further their career.

Part Two

The Bad

Chapter Four

Why Do We Have Bad Bosses?

In 1960, Douglas McGregor published a book called the <u>Human Side of Enterprise</u>[iii]. In this work, he examined two sets of beliefs that are held by those that lead others, which he called either Theory X or Theory Y. Those whose practices align with Theory Y believe that work comes naturally. Coercion is not necessary for people to perform their jobs. Self-direction comes naturally for people set to achieve ends to which they are committed. Being tasked with rewarding work is vital, and some of the highest rewards are those that give us a sense of satisfaction that we have accomplished something useful. People naturally learn, and as they grow they seek responsibility and challenges. They are capable of utilizing imagination, creativity, and ingenuity to accomplish their objectives. Many individuals find their intellectual capacity to be underutilized in their day-to-day work. They have the potential to use much more of their intellect to address the challenges that organizations face.

According to Theory X, people need to be coerced to meet their expectations. The natural condition is for people to do as little as possible to get by unless they are closely supervised. Because of their dislike for work, people need direction and control. If you turn your back on them, they will cheat or cut corners because they are lazy and apathetic. According to Theory X, people want to be directed and told what to do because they avoid taking responsibility at all costs and don't possess the ambition to grow.

I am describing these two theories because I believe that McGregor's work was the "grand-daddy" of them all when it comes to writings about leadership. I think that every study on leadership can trace its roots to McGregor's work. McGregor only reported these two beliefs—he didn't come down on the side of one or the other. He left it to others who followed him to make their own determination about what was good or bad. It's probably no surprise to you that the good bosses that I worked for were motivated by Theory Y and the bad bosses by Theory X.

In the over half-century since this book came out, one could probably do a doctoral dissertation on the number of books written on the subject of leadership as well as the dollars spent on leadership courses, assessment centers, and the salaries of management consultants, leadership trainers, and administrators who support such work. I have heard CEOs from organizations around the world articulate the virtues of Theory Y. It is behind every corporate value statement that I've ever read. After all of this, why do we still have so many bad bosses?

Over the years, I have been a part of (or made aware of) many meetings that take place with a senior leader, in which an HR person seeks funding for an incredibly expensive leadership program. Here is how this scenario generally plays out. The program will be designed to teach management how to lead to support the organization's strategic imperative, or something to that effect. With the force of dedication, the HR professional outlines the key learnings that will result from this program and describes the behaviors that program graduates will demonstrate as a result of attending. Over three days in a five-star resort, and while being pampered by an officious staff, the participants will gather, freeing themselves from the boundaries of their day-to-day work so that they can focus on the weighty issue of how to be a great leader.

Hearing the presentation is a glassy-eyed executive, thinking about the technical issues that his group is facing or about the weekly status report that he needs to provide to his boss or some equally critical tactical matter. Everybody in the room knows that the executive displays behaviors that are the polar opposite to what will be covered by the program. Moreover, the executive rewards and promotes subordinates for displaying the same behaviors as he does.

However, after the conclusion of the presentation, the executive offers a reflexive "well done," knowing that this will help him meet his KPI by ensuring that 75% of his leaders attend this program by year end. He fully understands that absolutely nothing is going to happen as a result, except that some consultant who is going to deliver the program is going to make a lot of money. After the meeting, the executive goes back to leading the same way he always has, satisfied that he will meet his KPI and ensure his year-end bonus.

Shortly after that, the leadership program kicks off, led by an HR leader who naively believes that this program will drive change in the organization. They hope it will spawn a new crop of leaders despite the unsupportive culture because this time, unlike many previous attempts, the participants will be highly motivated to implement their action plans. However after the program is over, the only thing that will be guaranteed is that the participants will be able to check the box that they met the KPI to attend.

Why does this wasted money continue to be spent? Why is it that after over one-half century of studies on what a good boss is and the impact of these people on positive results, that we still see no improvement in the number of good bosses that get promoted and the number of bad bosses that do? Organizations don't put bosses in leadership positions for the purpose of ensuring only mediocre performance. So why do organizations continue to produce bad bosses? Like any complex issue, there are no simple answers. There is a saying that "good bosses are made they aren't born," and I would argue the same is true for bad bosses as well.

Let's take a look at some of the more common reasons that bad bosses exist—I suggest that there are six main explanations:

Firstly, despite the available data, some obdurate decision makers refuse to believe in the linkage between the quality of a boss and performance. There is overwhelming evidence to show that good bosses drive excellent performance and bad bosses lead to mediocre performance. But such a belief is antithetical to the value system of certain decision makers. I will give you an example. At one point in my career, I was responsible for the implementation of a global leadership development process that consisted of several offerings targeted at various levels of management. The centerpiece of this process was a program that pulled in various senior leaders as part of the faculty. The instructor would teach a leadership skill; then, the senior leader would share how they had applied this skill through their own experiences by telling a story that had positive business results, highlighting how they had been successful as a result. For example, if the subject were win-win conflict resolution, the senior leader would tell a story of how he applied these techniques in resolving an actual conflict in the organization. The above process is a pretty sound method of instruction since it rules out the possible objection from course participants that "this would never work here."

One day, I received a phone call from one of the senior leaders who was part of our faculty. He informed me that he was dropping out of the program. He said that he received a phone call from a more (much more) senior leader, who informed him that his participation in this program would be detrimental to his career. He would be seen as "soft" because he was involved in such "nonsense" as these leadership programs. This senior leader had committed a potentially career-ending mortal sin because he strayed away from the micro-managing autocratic philosophy held by the organization's leaders.

Many times I have experienced or heard from others this disbelief in the value of the practices of good bosses. One of the ways that I have learned this is through the administration of 360-degree feedback. This process consists of a formal survey in which an individual receives feedback from all the people around him: boss, peers, subordinates, and customers (hence the name "360-degree"). These individuals receive feedback based upon a profile of a good boss that is designed explicitly by successful incumbent bosses in that organization. It is meant to evaluate the individual against leadership characteristics that are required to be successful. The higher that the feedback recipient scores, the closer they are to displaying the attributes of a good boss. I've done hundreds of these 360 processes over the years. I have seen a number of individuals who reject the feedback simply because they don't agree with the survey results. However they don't disagree with the accuracy of the feedback. Instead, they disagree with the value of it. "I manage this way because my boss wants me to, and that's how he manages me," is a typical reaction that I hear when someone reacts this way. In the feedback recipient's mind, who should he listen to: the survey results or his boss who has been successful in his career acting the opposite of how the survey says to behave? Place yourself in his shoes. Who is going to have a more significant impact on his career, the leadership survey or his boss? Every organization has both good and bad bosses, and it is very common for good bosses to design the success profile and for bad bosses to discount it.

Assuming that the feedback recipient who rejected this feedback is right and his boss is successful despite not displaying the leadership characteristics of a good boss, a key question to ask is how did this leader who took the survey wind up with a bad boss? The answer to this question leads us to the *second reason why we have bad bosses and that is that we tend to hire and promote people just like us*. A micro-managing autocrat is not going to hire a subordinate that brings creativity to his job and who likes to be empowered to do the best work he can. Instead, he is going to find a subordinate boss who wants to take orders and avoids responsibility or displaying initiative.

I contend that a bad boss can't develop a good boss. Why should he anyway, if a bad boss believes that the way that he leads others is the right way? When assigning work to his subordinates, the micro-managing autocratic boss is going to go with the team member that is the most likely to carry it out his instructions as directed, assuming that the technical ability is the same for all of his direct reports. The choice assignments will continue to go to this team member. Since this is usually where job development comes from, it is this compliant team member who receives the best development and, therefore, is likely to be put forward for promotion when the organization is selecting future leaders. Would you like to hazard a guess as to what type of boss this individual will make when he starts leading others? What were the leadership characteristics of the boss that mentored and rewarded him for compliant behavior?

I've done a lot of work with leaders over the years, helping them to make the right decision as to which of their subordinates should be selected or developed for future leadership positions. The toughest battle that I've had to fight with leaders is when they use current job performance as a way to determine future success in a leadership role of greater responsibility. It is especially difficult when the potential leader has never led anyone before, as there is little data to go on in making the decisions. The decision makers examine how an individual performed as an individual contributor and extrapolate on how they will function as a leader who will manage others who will do the work. In other words, it is thought that if they worked hard, were smart, paid attention to details, brought issues to closure promptly and communicated with their boss, then they will make a great boss. Now, those characteristics are good ones to have, and to a certain degree, they may be beneficial in leading others. However, they are not all you need when your responsibilities transition from doing the job yourself to beginning to do the job through others. Some individual contributors make this change to being the boss successfully and start doing management work. However, others do not, and they continue to act as an individual contributor even though they are now leading others.

The inability to make this transition to delivering through others is the third reason why bad bosses exist. An individual contributor is promoted to be the boss because he was smart, paid attention to details, brought issues to closure, and communicated upwards. Now, he is the boss, and he continues to do these things himself, rather than through his team members. In some ways, this problem is perfectly understandable. These individuals were recognized and rewarded for displaying a particular set of skills. Therefore, if the organization doesn't ask them to stop using these skills because they are now in a leadership position, aren't they likely to continue to use it?

Very few bosses start their careers in leadership roles. Instead, they begin as individual contributors who demonstrate excellent performance, get noticed, and earn a promotion. High performing individual contributors are known to get results by taking personal responsibility, overcoming obstacles, and showing dogged persistence and goal focus. In a leadership role, these very same qualities, if displayed the same way, could mean the boss overlooks the power of his team members to produce results and instead ends up either micro-managing them or doing the work himself.

Responding promptly and directly when a problem emerges is an admirable quality for an individual contributor. We all would want a first responder who possesses this quality, and they should be rewarded for displaying these characteristics. However, this reward comes at a price when these same individuals are promoted into leadership positions, as they sometimes are unable to let go. "Firefighting" can be a liability for a leader, if he is fighting the fires that are best done by team members. It is almost like an addiction: they experience an adrenaline rush from confronting a significant problem that only they can solve and euphoria from knowing that others have noticed their ability to "save the day."

I saw an example of this several years ago. I was associated with a senior leader for an organization who possessed the characteristic that I just described – a need to fight fires and "save the day." An example of this behavior occurred one Friday afternoon when the work was winding down for the week and he had nothing to do. During his tour he noticed a piece of wood laying across the yellow line marking the walkway, a clear safety violation. However, rather than bringing this to the attention of the area leader for a quick remedy, he called an immediate meeting of all direct report leaders, even those from other parts of the organization who weren't part of the area in question, bringing them to his conference room. He demanded an explanation and dictated the development of an action plan to remedy the problem, preventing just these occurrences in the future. Two hours after being called to the conference room, these leaders were dismissed.

His reaction could have been understandable if there was a track record of lax safety enforcement, but there wasn't. Instead, this was a pattern of behavior of the indispensable problem solver rising to the occasion and saving the day. Tackling tough problems head-on was what got this person promoted. It served him well early in his career. However, he was never able to shed this behavior as he rose to a senior level. His subordinates saw his action as overkill and a needless distraction as they could have easily handled the problem themselves. A simple phone call to the appropriate subordinate leader, reporting this safety issue, would have sufficed. However, because he inserted himself into this issue, overblowing the severity of it with his subordinate leaders, he ultimately reduced his respect in their eyes. But in his mind, he had risen to the occasion and saved the day.

It is not just strengths that can get us into trouble, weaknesses can too. There are times when bosses transition into a new role and they fail to understand what these weaknesses are and therefore look for ways to mitigate them. One of the characteristics that I have found in high performers is that they know what their weaknesses are and look for ways to mitigate them. These people recognize that as human beings, we inherently have weaknesses. As hard as we may try to improve, we will always have them. Sometimes these weaknesses lie dormant based upon the job situation. For example, two of my personal weaknesses are that I am stubborn and impatient. In periods where I'm driving needed changes, these weaknesses aren't as much of an issue. In fact, they could be strengths in that they enable me to get things done. However, in periods when I need to be very collaborative with peers, they can be a problem. In a position that requires me to be collaborative with peers all the time, I would have a significant problem succeeding since my default is to take action independently without input from others.

There are also times when organizations purposely place an individual in a leadership position and only want him to make the transition to the boss in job title alone. They want him to continue to display strong technical ability, taking away the decision-making authority from direct reports. They aren't interested in the leader's competence in his management responsibilities. There is someone in a more senior position who will handle those critical aspects of his job. In my experience, I've seen two reasons that organizations take such action. First, there is a belief that if you aren't technically competent in the stuff that your team members are doing, they will take advantage of you. Because people are generally lazy and apathetic, they will try to get away with not performing unless you clearly understand what they are doing so that you can closely monitor and control them. Your employees won't respect you unless you possess at least as much technical expertise as they have. They must be closely supervised and monitored for them to perform. This rationalization aligns with McGregor's Theory X.

The second reason that I've seen this happen is that in some organizations, I've seen leaders who don't understand the role of management; they are technical experts themselves and therefore believe that to succeed, one must follow in their footsteps. In my experience this is very commonplace in highly technical organizations where specialized expertise is part of the organization's core competence. Do not doubt, however, that if these organizations placed a higher premium on leadership in those who manage, the performance would be much better.

The fourth reason that we have bad bosses is that we put people into leadership roles who don't want to lead others. All too often, when management wants to pick a new boss, they look for the smartest, most highly educated and technically competent candidates. What leaders fail to see is that some individuals have honed their technical skills and picked up extra credentials because they want to practice in their chosen professional field and not to manage others. I've seen individual contributors enticed into leadership roles by higher pay, the corner office, and reserved parking. But all things being equal, they would rather do the work themselves as opposed to leading others. This type of individual sees himself as a highly compensated individual contributor. All that management stuff becomes an annoyance.

An example of this occurred in my career some years ago when I was trying to convince my boss that our team should offer a service to help leaders to become more effective at correcting performance problems. It seemed to me that this idea was a no-brainer, as senior management had highlighted this issue as an organization-wide problem—and one that they did not have a solution for. I thought that I had a solution in the form of this development process that we could deliver. I took the proposal to my boss to obtain his support in allowing me to take action. The solution would require my time, but little financial cost. I was receiving limited direction from him. I was fulfilling the responsibilities that he had already entrusted me with and could fold this into my existing workload, so I did not anticipate any resistance.

My boss thought that my solution was sound, and he agreed that there was indeed an organizational problem in this area. However, he didn't want me to proceed, as he needed more time to consider my proposal. It was not a priority for him. Over the next few weeks, I made repeated attempts to take up this issue for him to approve or reject it, all to no avail. Finally, he pulled me into his office and told me that nobody from senior management was asking our team to take care of this problem. Moreover, he said, "by you wanting me to get involved in this issue, you are pulling me away from my work to spend time and energy managing you." It wasn't that this boss thought what I was proposing wasn't a good solution or important to do. He told me that it sounded like a good idea. However, in the absence of being specifically directed by his boss to take action on this issue, he saw no reason to place any time or energy on it. In fact, he worried that maybe his boss wouldn't think that this was a good idea. He saw only a possible downside to supporting my request. Managing others was a burden, a distraction to what he wanted to spend time and energy on: carrying out the requests of his boss.

It may sound crazy that someone in a leadership role did not see the importance of the responsibility of leading others—such considerations only interfered with "his" work. In an organization where the leader's role is that of a glorified technician who happens to have people reporting to him, combined with having someone in a management position who doesn't actually want to lead others, this can easily happen.

The fifth most significant reason that we have bad bosses is because of the tight management control systems that seem to permeate so many organizations. Organizations put in place management control mechanisms such as governing policies and procedures and short-term metrics and KPIs, many of which measure non value-added activity as opposed to valued-added output. For example, the leadership program that I discussed earlier may measure how many people attended versus how many that attended obtained a tangible improvement in business performance as a result of the program. Other control systems that I have seen consist of multiple layers of excessive and redundant management that are responsible for managing two or more levels of bosses below them. A typical example of this is the practice of having a two-level management signoff before any money on an annual performance rating is determined.

Organizations with rigorous control systems create bad bosses in two ways. First, they make it challenging to develop good bosses. The best development for good bosses is a healthy dose of assignments that contain significant responsibilities. The leaders that I interviewed reinforced this to me, as their success resulted from being given these kinds of projects. These important developmental experiences included high expectations for results and a lot of latitude to act as they thought best. Turning around a failing organization or starting up a new operation were among the valuable assignments that these leaders were given.

In an organization with robust management control systems, bosses are denied the latitude to figure things out on their own, because they are micro-managed. Governing policies and procedures turn them into automatons. It's "management by the numbers": follow the system and you can't fail. If the more challenging, high expectations assignments do exist, there can't be enough of them to develop all the future leaders that require it. These organizations end up promoting people into positions of responsibility and expecting them to make decisions and take action when they have no experience in this. Imagine a child that is raised by parents who have given him everything, made all his decisions for him and never expected him to take responsibility. What will happen to him when he leaves home and strikes out on his own?

The second way that these controlling systems create problems is that they make it difficult for bad bosses to get found out. In an environment where leaders are expected to be technically competent, keep higher levels of management informed and manage to short-term goals and KPIs, there tends to be little difference between mediocre and excellent performance. I say this because the control systems that these organizations put into place are there so that individuals don't take initiative or display creativity that is necessary to excel. In essence, this means mediocrity is the target. Excellent performance is obscured. Let's go back to the example of the leadership development program. The KPI was first to deliver the program and to ensure that people attended. Let's suppose for the sake of the argument that we have a good boss and a bad boss who both send their team members to the program. Therefore, both get a check mark for meeting the objective. What if the good boss goes further and ensures that the action plans are implemented, by providing challenging development assignments and feedback? This good boss may get a warm feeling knowing that he will positively impact organizational performance in the future by increasing the capacity of his people to lead effectively. However, in the eyes of the organization, both bosses met the objective. It would be different if the KPI were something more meaningful as *developing good bosses* instead of *program attendance*. However, the former is very subjective, where the latter is objective and, therefore, easy to measure. Most control systems depend on objective measures designed to measure the result, but not the process to achieve that result. The boss that micro-manages subordinates to achieve results or the incompetent boss who happens to have a very talented team working for him that produces the expected result, despite poor leadership, look the same as the boss who encourages people to work smarter.

I remember a discussion with a senior leader who reflected on the organizational control systems that "guided" his life at work. He lauded them because, in his words, they protected him from failing. This leader talked in glowing terms about how, whenever he needed to take on a crucial challenge, there was a policy and procedure that explained what he needed to do and how he needed to do it. If he followed the process, he would stay out of trouble. If there were a failure, it certainly wouldn't be his fault. It was the procedure that failed. I call it management by the numbers. If you follow the policies and procedures to the letter, you will never fail. However, it comes with a price. Essential characteristics of high performers such as initiative, risk taking, continuous improvement, and creativity are discouraged, if not punished.

The sixth reason that we have bad bosses is that many organizational leaders who make decisions about who are the future bosses give this selection process short shrift. Specifically, they haven't thought through what criteria they are using to make these selection decisions. Or, they want to spend as little time as possible on this process. There is a tendency to focus on easy to identify criteria such as intelligence, educational credentials, hard work, and being personally able to achieve results. This happens instead of looking at more difficult to discern characteristics such as empowering and developing others, driving team members to continually improve performance, and empathy, all of which are displayed by good bosses. It is empathy that I have found to be the least considered characteristic of leadership.

I have always seen empathy as necessary, but my consideration of this quality was taken to a new level after reading a book on the Nuremberg war criminal trials called Nuremberg Diary, by G.M. Gilbert[iv]. Gilbert was a psychologist who was assigned to study the trial's defendants. His job was to ensure that they remained mentally healthy to stand trial. Through his analysis, Gilbert found that the defendants were all intelligent, some were evenly border-line geniuses. He also found something else: they all were incapable of empathy. Now, I've never known a boss who could be considered a war criminal. However, I have witnessed senior organization leaders select individuals for leadership positions who were highly intelligent and devoid of empathy. This disdain for empathy became apparent to me early in my career. I once led a project that was analyzing the most critical skills that effective bosses needed to display. The idea was that once we understood what these critical skills were, we could then use them as a basis to develop and select future leaders. As a part of this project, I surveyed dozens of successful incumbent bosses and asked them to rank order a list of possible skills or abilities that leaders should possess. Empathy made the list of the top ten, according to the survey participants. When I shared the list with senior leaders, they objected to empathy even being considered, despite the scientific nature of the study and what their experts had said. To them, empathy was a sign of weakness. If a leader displayed this attribute, he would be "used and manipulated" by his team members.

I have found that organizations use intelligence as a method to select leaders more than any other criteria. It is relatively easy to identify, and there is some science linking it to leadership success. Specifically, the ability to see the big picture and to conceptualize large scale change efforts are ways that successful bosses display intelligence. However, when I question leaders as to how a boss displays his intelligence, I usually receive answers that focus on different characteristics. Instead, what I hear is that he can learn a lot of complex information quickly, provide reasonable solutions to complex problems, and has acquired a lot of technical expertise. These are good qualities to have, for an individual contributor. These aren't the qualities that I would want to use in selecting a future leader. They could even be a detriment. I have seen many bright leaders use their intelligence to solve problems that their team should be addressing.

Along with using the wrong criteria for selection, I've seen senior leaders treat the selection of future leaders in a casual way, spending little time and effort at it, overly simplifying a complicated process. The time allocation is less than the time they would spend on rehearsing a significant presentation that they are making to senior leaders. When I suggest a more robust process, I sometimes hear comments such as, "I'm a good judge of picking future leaders. After all, I'm a good leader, so I'll pick someone like me." Challenging these leaders with a metric for selecting good bosses that does not match with the way that they themselves behave, can be like presenting them with a bitter pill to swallow. These leaders may find it easier to discount a proven quality process than to consider that their own behavior may not be ideal. A bad boss may not want to tell his organization that they need to start selecting leaders who act the opposite to the way that he behaves.

Bad bosses will always be with us. I wish that I could say that we are winning the battle and improving the quality of the leaders, but it's not happening. We need the excellent performance that strong leaders bring out of our organizations, now more than ever, to compete in the global economy. However, I have not seen a significant shift in organizational thinking that would yield such a change in how we think about leadership any time soon. Selecting bosses is a complex and challenging process. Even those organizations that take the selection process seriously struggle with it since no method is foolproof. Even the best processes will sometimes yield a bad boss. Therefore, waiting for someone to take care of your bad boss for you is a fruitless course of action. Beginning with the next chapter, we'll get into how to deal with these bad bosses when you find yourself in a position of working for one.

Chapter Five

How Does Your Boss Respond to Conflict?

In this chapter, we will examine the issue of conflict and how the boss responds to it. For this exercise, I'm going to expand the definition of conflict and take into consideration the handling complicated issues such as objections to workplace changes, building consensus, delivering valuable feedback, and holding people accountable. In essence, for the purposes of this discussion conflict will include anything that requires the boss taking a position that could create some disagreement or resistance from others.

Good bosses, as a default, approach conflict in a way such that both sides can meet their needs, even in times of conflict, when the boss may hold all the power. In the example that I used with my boss when I was fifteen, he had all of the power to fire me on the spot, and I would have had no recourse, and I knew this because I had seen him do this to others. However, he approached our discussion with a different focus. Looking at things from his perspective, he had invested in me and saw how his business could capitalize on this investment if my behavior changed. For me, if I improved, I could keep the job that I wanted and, in the future, take on new assignments that I would enjoy. What I just described is known as "win-win" in conflict negotiation parlance.

There are, of course, other ways that bosses could resolve conflict, such as compromise, where both sides give up something to reach an agreement. The problem can be that often the fix is temporary or so watered-down that is rendered unworkable for either side. Other bosses tend to use win-lose, where they will focus on winning at all costs, thus alienating themselves from the losers. There is also lose-win, although, with all of my experience, I can't say that I've seen this style practiced by many bosses. Those that do sure don't stay around very long. You can usually work with the bosses who engage in the forms of conflict resolution styles that I have just outlined. The last method of handling conflict is avoiding it altogether, which is a lose-lose. In other words, this boss suppresses conflict. For example, he may neglect to provide harsh feedback to a subordinate that is needed for that individual to perform better. It's not even delivering the bad news that can stymy this boss. Sometimes it can also even be good news that will place him in a position where he might have to take a position that he wants to avoid.

To illustrate this point, let's take a look at an example from my personal experience with such a boss. Several years ago, one beautiful morning, I was in the men's room, standing there taking care of business and contemplating the design of the tile work on the wall in front of me. Just as I began this process, my boss came in and stood beside me to take care of the same "business" that brought me there. He then began to inform me that he had just approved my performance appraisal rating, which was relatively high—a pleasant surprise for me. As we were washing and drying our hands, he shared with me the amount of my annual increase and bonus that would accompany it. I contemplated offering a handshake in appreciation; however, in the current circumstances, it didn't seem appropriate. Leaving the room, with me behind him, he told me to keep up the excellent work. In 90 seconds, he handled the pressing business that brought him to the room to begin with, and also told me what he thought about the last year of my work, and he treated both activities with the same amount of enthusiasm.

What was the message that he conveyed to me during that short interaction? Based upon studies of human interaction, when we receive communication from a sender, we tend to focus on how the delivery of the message as opposed to what was said. When I yell at my cat for clawing the sofa, and he runs away after scolding him, I don't think that he understands the verbiage. Instead, he knows that he gets yelled at when he decides to sharpen his claws improperly. He reacts to my loud voice and not the words themselves.

In my case, my boss chose a setting that was best suited to talk about the highlights of last night's ball game and used it to tell me what he honestly thought about me. He didn't do this by the words he used. The message I got was that he didn't care about me enough to have a proper discussion, rather this was a perfunctory duty that held equal standing with the biological need that compelled him to the men's room in the first place. The annual increase that I received was one of the most sizable ever, and it was a near-perfect appraisal rating—this was indeed an occasion to celebrate. He could have used this event as an opportunity to reinforce what I did well to ensure that it would continue in the future. We could have entered this discussion together with the energy and goodwill from the rating and income increase that I had just received, and used it to ensure a strong level of commitment to even higher levels of performance. All he needed to do was to spend a couple of minutes preparing, choose a different venue, and take a few more minutes for this conversation. This small time investment is a low price to pay for the potential gain in performance that a proper feedback discussion could provide. Who knows what he would have done if he hadn't found me in the men's room at the same time? At least he had the courtesy to check to see that we were alone. If he handles good news this way, you can imagine how he might deliver bad news such as telling someone that he was underperforming.

Why did he do this? Admittedly, at an intellectual level, he knew that this was not the best practice. He wasn't new to the process of performance appraisal. He had been part of discussions with senior leaders on how to give a proper one. As the HR head, I had implemented this very system a few months before organization-wide, with his full support (or at least he said that he supported it). The reason he gave such short shrift to the development discussion was because challenging me to higher levels of performance or to brainstorming ideas on what I could have done differently would have required taking a position. I might have said that I didn't think that I could do more than I was doing today, or perhaps I may have thought that my rating should have been even higher. Those reactions from me would have placed him in a position where he would feel uncomfortable. Taking a stand is anathema to someone who avoids conflict. This sort of behavior from this boss was not new; I had seen it from the very beginning.

I joined this organization following an extensive interview process with both the head of the organization and the leader of the organizational change process, to whom I reported directly. When I joined, I reported to the head of Administration and Organizational Change. He, in turn, reported to the organization head, who had an exciting and challenging vision of what he wanted the organization to be in the future. My new boss was responsible for carrying this vision out. I was tasked with building the HR organization and supporting the implementation of this vision. This meant that, in effect, I worked directly for the organization head when working on bringing his vision to reality.

Once I came on board, I began to see how the organization head and my boss operated. The head left it up to my boss to be "the heavy," which meant confronting his peers, the other direct reports to the organization head, to support the change process that he was leading. However, this confrontation spilled over into other areas as well. He confronted individuals over performance concerns that seemed unrelated to the change process that he was leading. As you would expect, his peers didn't appreciate this usurpation of power and were openly complaining about it to the organization head. They were also sharing their concerns with me.

Six weeks after I joined the organization, my boss was fired by the organization head. My now ex-boss called me after the event, expressing surprise, as he no idea that this was coming. My boss was thrown under the proverbial bus, as it was clear that the organization's head had never told my now discredited boss about the complaints that he was receiving. Shortly after the call, the organization head called me into his office and told me the full story; that the termination was due to the lack of support from peers. I was going to take over the change process responsibilities, in addition to my HR role, and report directly to him. I was now in the position to pick up where my just-fired ex-boss had left off. I had some concerns since I certainly didn't want to end up like him.

Over the next few weeks, I began to understand the relationship that the organization head had with my now ex-boss. He was open about his concerns with his direct reports, my new peers. These were the same concerns shared by my ex-boss. What I found somewhat disturbing is that although he had an excellent understanding of the issues regarding my ex-boss's relationship with peers, he took no action to prevent it by giving him the feedback that could have turned the situation around. He may have interviewed me with my ex-boss's termination in mind. There was also no feeling of remorse over not sharing the feedback. He simply let the issue build. I began to wonder whether he had thought about what would eventually happen - did he believe that the problems were merely going to go away?

The longer I worked for him, the more I gained a clearer picture of my new boss. I could see that he was brilliant and highly educated in addition to having good visionary ideas that would positively impact the organization's future. This boss spent almost his entire career as an individual contributor and lacked leadership experience, especially the kind of experience that would have prepared him for this role. When it came to operationalizing his vision, things began to break down. He operated by providing general direction. He disdained to offer specifics about what he wanted team members to do to support the organizational change that was taking place, informing me that he hired these people because they were smart and experienced enough to know what to do. He felt he shouldn't have to provide them with specific direction. Job-related feedback was also off the list for him; this was especially the case when he determined that a team member was avoiding action that they should take or taking action that they shouldn't. He now put me in the position of delivering this difficult feedback for him, just like he had expected of my now-disgraced ex-boss. I dutifully did what I was asked and had discussions with each affected direct report. However, my efforts only served as a band-aid, as the real problem was a lack of proper communication between the organization head and his team members.

As months turned into years, I continued to provide feedback to peers the best I could. It is hard to provide specific feedback to a peer second-hand from a boss who very often is vague about what he wants. Frequently, the discussion was something like, "the boss is dissatisfied with what is going on in your shop." Terminations and demotions became the order of the day under this boss, who was intolerant of a lack of performance. Each of these individuals had been very successful in their previous role before they came to work for this boss; now, they were sub-par performers.

As the head of HR, I was part of these disciplinary processes. Each of these individuals was bitter and had not received feedback from their boss about not meeting his expectations. Many of them thought that they had been doing fine because any interactions that they had were reasonably positive. Even though they had been getting some signals of dissatisfaction from other surrogates like me, the boss hadn't been expressing dissatisfaction, so they felt that any concerns weren't really serious. It would have been possible to correct these performance problems if the organization head had been able to have meaningful discussions about his concerns.

It was clear that this boss was passive aggressive. He harbored his concerns about others, but muted those concerns in vague language designed to encourage improvement rather than give authentic feedback. It wasn't that he never expressed his opinions with others openly. Rather, he would hold onto his frustrations until he could retain them no more, and they would come out in a fit of anger, like a dam bursting. In these cases, his angry words lacked the clarity of specificity so that all the receiver got was unproductive emotion and no helpful feedback. For example, one of the goals that he assigned to me, which was a rare occurrence, was to implement a significant HR practice. In one of our meetings, I shared with him some of the resistance that I was receiving. He blew up at me and blamed me for not pushing through the opposition; it was a problem that was mine to work through. However, I was merely informing him of the status since I knew that this project was essential to him. He later came back and apologized for his overreaction.

Although this boss was reticent to give direct feedback for his concerns on significant issues, he was much more open about doing this for petty matters. Reprimanding me for a poorly constructed email was an excellent example of this. One day, sitting at my desk, I opened a message from this boss, replying to an email that I sent him the day before. His email consisted of a scathing critique of my original text, highlighting several grammatical errors and run-on sentences. He was right; the email was hastily done and contained errors, but his reaction was overblown. He went out of his way to point out the errors and in fact didn't even respond to the question in the email which needed a response. This grammar lesson continued for some weeks. The smallest error would be fed back to me in his response. I found that I was not the only one who was having this experience; other team members received the same treatment. These were the same individuals for whom the boss had already expressed to me his dissatisfaction. Therefore, I began to believe that I was also on the list of individuals that he was dissatisfied with, and the issue wasn't really my poorly worded emails. In the absence of direct feedback, I surmised his dissatisfaction with me was because of my inability to change the behavior of his subordinates. Knowing that he would be able to construct a dubious criticism of me for something that he was unwilling or unable to do, he instead channeled his frustration against an issue that would be difficult for me to defend—the poorly constructed email.

One incident in particular was the proverbial last straw. One of my responsibilities was to prepare senior leaders for an annual review of talent for presentation to the overall organization head—this was the person to whom my boss reported. Also in attendance would be the organization head of HR to whom I reported on a dotted-line basis. The purpose of this review was to discuss critical positions, who the successors were for these roles, and to identify high potentials who could fill higher level jobs in other parts of the entire organization. According to the overall organization head, one of the boss's direct reports was as a high potential. For our purposes, I will refer to this individual as Leader X. Leader X was intelligent and ambitious, both well-educated and articulate, and not at all unlike my boss. My boss supported this individual as a high potential for two reasons. First, he knew that the overall head of the organization, his boss, viewed him as a high potential, and he sure wasn't going to challenge that view. Second, and most importantly, my boss wanted to get rid of Leader X, who had a history of both being resistant to change and an unable to get along with fellow staff members.

I had also had dealings with Leader X, specifically in helping him implement a critical HR initiative, designed to support the organizational vision that was so critical to our boss. The boss asked me to get involved personally. He didn't want to take a firmer hand in driving this change because of Leader X's typical resistant attitude. True to form, my collaboration with Leader X was rocky, with many starts and stops. I had no real power to get Leader X to move faster. He raised objections that I resolved only to be replaced by other concerns. I shared my experience with this sort of "stone-walling" with the boss, who simply shook his head. He was too afraid to confront Leader X because of this person's known propensity to argue and resist when confronted, and as we have discussed my boss had a natural reluctance to confront issues head-on.

During the annual review with the overall head of the organization Leader X was asked about the status of this HR initiative since it involved filling some very strategic positions with some of the organization's high potentials. In reply, Leader X lied and said he was waiting for direction from HR to be able to take action, basically making me the scapegoat. I was shocked to see that my boss said nothing to defend me. After the meeting, I confronted my boss and he agreed that Leader X had told a lie, but promised no action to remedy the situation. He couldn't face Leader X because of his conflict avoidant style. He wasn't going to tell his boss the truth since that would raise questions about his leadership and Leader X's qualifications for higher level responsibilities. The best course of action in his mind was to throw me under the bus, as I was the expendable one. It was at this moment that I decided that it was time for me to leave this boss. I had waited too long to take action that I should have taken much earlier in my career with him, and now I was paying the price. I began the process of leaving this organization.

I was in the final stage of my job search when it came time for my next performance review. The performance discussion with my boss started pretty well. We sat down and reviewed each of my objectives and how I performed against the targets. I was impressed by the quality of the feedback. I even had thoughts that perhaps things were finally turning around. He ended the discussion by summarizing that he saw my performance as excellent. However, before he could give a final rating, he would need to seek feedback from the overall head of HR because of my dotted line reporting relationship to him. This was the proper procedure. After obtaining the additional input, I looked forward to an excellent final report.

About two weeks later, I saw an email from the boss with the completed and signed-off appraisal attached. Sending it to me in this way was a clear violation of our organization's practices, which he knew, since the results were meant to be delivered face to face. More surprising, however, was that my final rating was 180 degrees different than the earlier discussion. My score was below average. My boss lacked the courage to present this change to me face to face; instead, he left me to open this "gift" on my own. After printing the appraisal, I walked the 100 feet to his office and requested an audience. The only explanation that he could give me was: "It wasn't me that did this. Headquarters HR doesn't think that you are giving the organization and me the support that I need."

Did he string me on in our first meeting and decided to let headquarters be the "bad guy?" Or, was he honest with me, but lacked the courage to stand up to headquarters and disagree with their evaluation? I guess that it was the latter—he couldn't exactly tell them that I was trying to help him and that it was *he* who wouldn't confront the lack of performance in others. I'm sure that the incident with Leader X weighed heavily in on their decision. In a sense, the headquarters group was right: I couldn't help him do what he wanted me to do in confronting others. I couldn't do his job for him. However, the real underlying problem was an inability to promote honest and transparent feedback on expectations. Nobody can succeed under a boss who keeps subordinates in the dark on ever-shifting expectations, who withholds valuable feedback or won't confront poor behavior in team members, especially when that behavior is unethical (as in the case of Leader X's lie). You may think these are pretty basic expectations for a boss, and you are right. However for a passive-aggressive boss, they are beyond his capacity. A few days later, I returned the signed performance appraisal along with my letter of resignation, as I had accepted a job offer from another organization.

I blame myself for this issue because I stayed too long under this boss, a mistake that I promised myself that I would not repeat. I had an opportunity to apply lessons learned a few years later with another boss who couldn't handle conflict. In this new example, my reporting relationship, role, and responsibilities were similar to the previous case. I worked with the organization head to implement a new HR practice that would improve the process of identifying future leaders. Primarily, it would promote more transparency and planning for a process that lacked rigor. About two weeks after the change was approved, and before its implementation, the organization head decided to take early retirement. His position was backfilled by a boss from another part of the organization. I sat down with my new boss and reviewed the impending change and his role in this process. I detected that he did not view it favorably based upon his facial expressions and lack of supportive verbal cues. He seemed to shut down. Reading these cues, I asked him point blank if he would like me to postpone this implementation. A quick decision was required, as the annual cycle was fast approaching. He informed me that I should continue with the implementation, which I did.

From the very beginning, the implementation was a disaster. I began to hear from others who had more open relationships with this boss that he didn't like the process at all. As I began to know this boss more, it was clear as to why the open and transparent process that I was implementing was anathema to his very value system. He didn't want the transparency, because it put the decision-making process out in the open. This process was previously performed behind closed doors and had a reputation for arbitrary decisions that produced ineffective leaders. At the time that I shared the plans for the change with him he already knew that he didn't like them. However, he chose not to be honest with me because of his adverse conflict style; rather, he let it fail. If he had tried to stop this implementation, he would be telling me that he wanted to continue to make these arbitrary decisions. Instead, he avoided the issue but then refused to use the new system when it was rolled out, thus ensuring the process was stillborn. Weeks' worth of work went down the drain. There was also an erosion of HR's credibility in the eyes of our customers. A simple "no" from this boss would have prevented this damaging result.

On top of all this, it was clear that he was angry with me as he reduced the number of opportunities for us to interact and even used intermediaries to transmit his instructions to me as opposed to facing me directly. The situation was far from ideal and one day I reached my limit. As background to the story, I had been asked by one of his direct reports to assist in implementing an HR initiative in his area. Providing this support had been common practice and I had engaged in it many times during my tenure. A few days after I participated in this effort, I received a call from the organization head. He was angry and demanded an explanation as to why I had been involved without seeking his permission first. I informed him that this had been a common practice for quite a while and that I was unaware that he wanted me to take up his time with such a request. What I was doing was simply helping leaders to think through an important decision that they needed to make. After venting his anger, he hung up. It was clear that he didn't want to solve the problem, just to let his emotions out. The issue itself was minor compared to his overreaction and called to mind the overblown tirades I had faced from my previous passive-aggressive boss over my emails. It seemed clear that he was expressing built-up anger due to his inability to address the critical problems that I had raised weeks before when it was time to decide whether to proceed with the roll-out of the process change to identify future leaders.

At this point I had been working for this person for about three months. I saw a repeat of the same behaviors that I experienced with the first boss: an inability to be direct when it was required, which allowed the organization to suffer as a result, and an overreaction to small incidents to express his dissatisfaction. Not wanting to repeat past mistakes, I considered my next moves. I checked with trusted others who had more knowledge about this boss in previous roles. They told me that they had seen many past examples of the type of behavior that I described. I realized that it was time to go and fast. I was gone within a few weeks, as I decided to take advantage of an opportunity in another part of the organization.

These types of leaders avoid dealing with severe issues or providing difficult but needed feedback. They may freely express concerns with trusted others, but not directly with the most relevant person when it may cause an unwanted conflict. They will focus on petty issues to an extreme as a way to exert their authority in a way that feels safe for them. Average bosses do things right, but good bosses do the right things, as the old saying goes. Every good boss that I've ever worked for has taken a stand to defend one or more of his people and ensure fairness. Every bad boss that I've worked for has avoided this type of conflict.

Some would say that two bosses that I've described in this chapter would eventually derail, that no leader could succeed in the long term because of the weaknesses that they possess. You might be able to simply wait them out. In both of these cases, the bosses had high-level sponsors who wanted them in these positions because they were bright, highly credentialed, and dependable. These sponsors were willing to overlook their other weaknesses. In the meantime, I witnessed wrecked careers during their tenure. I suggest taking action and managing your career as opposed to hoping that the organization will wise up and move them out. Although I survived, I suffered sleepless nights and much wasted unproductive effort trying to figure out how to meet their enigmatic expectations. What would my career have been like if I had left the boss in the first example earlier? At the least I probably would have been able to spend that energy much more productively.

The Conflict-Avoidant Boss	
How This Boss Behaves	**The Impact on You**
Lack of comfort or absolute avoidance of providing feedback—even if the message is positive.	Since you aren't receiving corrective feedback, you may be heading for a poor performance review or even job jeopardy. If you aren't receiving positive feedback, you may not know, in your boss's mind, what strengths you can further leverage or what tasks to focus on that your boss sees as important.
Feedback that you should have received is shared with others.	By going behind your back, at a minimum it shows that this boss does not respect you. At a maximum, it speaks to his lack of character. If this problem persists, it reduces both your chances of being seen a good performer in this boss's eyes and your job satisfaction.
Lack of direction on important issues.	By not knowing what is important to this boss, you may be focusing on things that aren't important and neglecting things that are. Over time this creates job jeopardy.
Over reaction to issues that don't warrant it.	Although the issue that creates concern with this boss may not be important, his reaction may be symptomatic of a deeper issue that is creating dissatisfaction that could impair your career with this boss. You need to find that out quickly and make a decision whether this issue can be addressed or if it is unsolvable.
Focus on petty issues.	If you are receiving clear direction on issues that are peripheral to your performance and not on important issues; then you run the risk of placing too much time and energy on the wrong things. This focus

	would be at the detriment of the right things, thus creating jeopardy to achieving your goals and objectives.

Chapter Six

How Does Your Boss Respond to Change?

The only constant in the world of work is change. I certainly have seen that over the 45 years of my career. This is true at an organization level; however, I've seen it a team level as well. I have seen teams flourish and grow because a good boss possessed a vision in alignment with the challenges faced by the entire organization and facilitated positive change that supported it. Conversely, I've seen teams cease to be relevant because the boss in charge of that group was resistant to positive change, even in the face of feedback from the organization that saw a reduced value in his team's performance. The bottom line is good bosses know where the organization is heading and without being asked, work with their team to develop a plan that helps the entire organization to achieve the future state that it desires. They aren't afraid of change and see it as a natural part of our work lives, just as it is in our personal lives.

The various bosses that I worked for had very different reactions to needed change. In some cases, these bosses appropriately coached and guided me through the change process, as I outlined in Chapter Two. In other cases, they were cheerleading from the sidelines. However, there were times when I worked for bosses who had a very adverse reaction to the change that I was implementing or seeking. Their negativity was not just towards the bigger picture "macro" changes that would improve team performance, but also to the small changes that required a simple decision. I've seen bad bosses who, as a default, avoid making decisions, usually out of fear of making the wrong one. They operate mired in a belief that it is far better not to decide than to risk a choice, because there is a chance that a senior leader may question that decision. And they lack the conviction to either defend that choice to senior management or accept censure where deserved. Not making a decision is the best way to avoid getting into trouble with their boss. In this chapter, we'll examine bad bosses who avoid making changes and the impact that this will have on your career.

I once had a boss who had an adverse reaction to a change that he hired me to make. In this example, I was employed by an organization to support a behavior change program. This program, which had been rolled out just before me joining, was designed to teach individuals to be more proactive, focus on continuous improvement, and to promote team member involvement in decision making. This behavior change program was part of a more significant performance improvement effort that was led by the organization's head. The true motivation for implementing this change was that he wanted to show senior leaders that he was strategic enough to be promoted into a senior position.

For the last 20 years, this organization head had to deal with operational problems in various parts of the business. He had a reputation as a firefighter who tackled and solved severe problems like turning around operations in trouble or launching new start-ups. This type of work came with a price as he relocated his family about every two years. You can imagine what his family life was like with all of that moving and the ongoing trauma of uprooting the kids from their schools and friends.

In a sense, he was a victim of his success. Whenever there was a trouble spot that needed someone with a firm hand to take control and to remedy the situation, he was the leader that the organization sought out. Once he fixed that problem, he was sent to another spot to start the process all over again. How could he develop the strategic ability needed for a more senior position, when he spent such a short time at each troubled spot? Senior leaders rewarded him for being a firefighter. Now, these same leaders were telling him that if he wanted a promotion, he would need to change to be more strategic.

He was nearing the end of his career journey. There was a job opening up at headquarters that would be a significant promotion, and he was a contender for the opportunity. To take on this more senior role, he needed to demonstrate that he could be more strategic. He felt that if he were successful, this would establish his bona fides and provide his pathway to promotion. I was hired to handle this change effort that was to be his last "big push."

In the first phase of the change process, which was implemented among first-line leaders, the behavior change worked well. The participants, by and large, appreciated the learning. Some exciting things came out of this experience, whereby the process participants implemented some meaningful projects that senior leaders could hold up as visible evidence of success. However, none of these projects was big enough to challenge the organizational status quo.

After about six months, it was now time to initiate phase two, which was for mid-level leaders. These were the bosses of the first-level leaders who went through phase one. Senior leaders had decided to roll out this process from the bottom up instead of the top down. My suggestion would have been to work from the top down, but the decision had already been made before I joined the organization. Mid-level leaders experienced the same learning as their first-level leaders, plus some teaching on their new role in the transformed organization which required them to take on more leadership responsibility. Traditionally, this organization had been very much engaged in top-down decision making. Therefore, this layer of management was very much used to simply relaying orders from on high to first-level leaders. One of the objectives of the process was to get this mid-level leadership layer to stand up and take responsibility for moving the organization forward and improving performance, not to wait for senior leadership to provide direction.

Following the training, in order to put this into practice, the mid-level leadership team decided to begin to meet every Friday at lunchtime for a couple of hours to discuss what tasks they were going to take on to improve the organization and to empower their team members. This group elected one of their peers to lead the team. I was to be the team's facilitator. Very quickly, the discussion turned to questions such as: why should we manage first-level leaders differently from the way that senior leaders manage us? How can I empower my first-level leaders to do a task that I, as their boss, am not authorized to perform? There was a strong tendency in this organization towards micromanaging. I witnessed, on many occasions, that this group of leaders was not allowed to make decisions on actions for areas that they were held responsible for, thus giving them the responsibility without the authority. I had built a good rapport with many of the team members and had a pretty good understanding of how the organization operated. Decision making took place at the highest levels, which made it complicated to roll out this effort from the bottom up. In essence, the organization head had asked the mid-level management to take responsibility and to lead. Still, he didn't provide them with the authority that they needed to carry that responsibility out. In Chapter Four, I described an incident where a group of leaders was called to a conference room to discuss corrective action because a senior leader found a piece of wood in a walkway. That anecdote took place in this same organization, and this group of leaders was also the same group summoned to the conference room.

As the program leader, as charged by senior management, I was now the messenger responsible for informing these managers about what they needed to do to make this process successful. What the senior leaders didn't envision was that they would have actually to change their behavior, too. This program made a lot of sense to senior leadership when the intention was for lower level leaders to change and be more productive. However, it became another thing entirely when this senior team realized that they needed to change their behavior, give up control, and empower their team members. As I began discussing the direction that the mid-level leadership team was taking, you could see the apprehension building in the minds of the senior leaders, especially those of the organization head.

Around this time, word came down that the coveted headquarters position opened up because the incumbent retired. However, the job went to a younger and more strategic leader. When I met with the organization head after this news came out, you could visibly see his sense of resignation. He would retire in the job he was in now, the responsibilities for which he could do in his sleep. I remember going into his office for an early morning meeting. He would have a newspaper spread out on his desk and would peruse it while he was talking to me, showing only a mild interest in what I was telling him about. Whether he realized it or not, he was sending me a signal that he didn't care anymore about what I was saying.

As I passed along the feedback that managers wanted more autonomy to make decisions, you could see the backpedaling begin. The organization head met with the team to discuss their issues. Taking their concerns into consideration, he thanked them for their hard work, but that was about the extent of his response. It was clear that nothing was going to get done. This inadequate response had a definite impact on the management team. The organization head had been hit with the realization that he would have to give up control and practice himself what he was asking his team members to do. However he couldn't change—it was beyond his ability and motivation. Although the team continued to meet, the motivation and energy were no longer there. Hired to support a change process that existed in name only, I started to see the end coming for my time working for this boss.

Supporting this change process was only one of my duties, the rest of which tended to be more administrative, and which I could do in my sleep. Deprioritizing the change process meant that my role and its value to this organization became hugely diminished. Even if I stayed, I didn't want to end up in a position where I would be the one reading a newspaper while meeting with one of my team members. I was too early in my career to allow it to stall. This organization hired a skill that I had, the ability to help organizations through change, and it was a skill that was no longer wanted. I decided that I couldn't stay and began to find an opportunity at headquarters where I would be valued. Within a few months, I was gone from this organization, working in a new role that challenged me.

Years later, I worked with another boss who had a similar aversion to change. In this role, I assumed the leadership responsibilities for a new talent management process in a very traditional and bureaucratic organization. I was responsible for rolling this out organization-wide, which included all of the education, infrastructure, and leadership support.

My new boss had been in his job for about six months, following a promotion from being one of the team members. The organization had decided to fill the position with the team member who possessed the best educational credentials and intelligence. The decision makers weren't concerned about leadership experience, of which he had little. The organization wasn't really looking for a good boss, either. Instead, what the organization head wanted was someone who would respond to his need for information on people, answering requests like "I'm thinking about promoting this person. Provide me with his performance appraisal information, and his talent assessment results." In other words, the organization saw my boss's role as that of a glorified individual contributor administrator. The organization didn't seem to care how well he would lead his team, let alone how strategic he was. Based on that criteria, they sure hired the right guy.

This boss could have delegated these lower-level administrative tasks to team members and, in turn, focused on the work of a senior leader, such as developing strategy, growing the capacity of team members to perform at higher levels of performance, or process improvement. However, he decided to forgo these critical challenges and fill this individual contributor role himself. He knew that he could control his own performance, so why take a chance on the performance of an employee? They might mess up the task and it would look bad on him. The fear of failure outweighed the gains of appropriately delegating functions that were really beneath him but that would allow him to focus on higher level issues befitting his leadership level.

This boss switched the management of the group to autopilot. All of the team members were experienced and had well-defined tasks when this boss took over, so everything worked well for a few months. However, after that, things started to break down. Some team members left because they didn't like the way that the boss abdicated his leadership, while others retired. Over time, as team members left the organization and new people came on board, his style became a problem. Finding themselves working for a boss who provided little or no direction while only focusing on his "own" responsibilities, the new team members struggled to find their way and thrive.

Initially my responsibilities with the implementation of the new talent management process did not overlap in such a way that this person's lack of management was an issue. However, once this process was up and running, I found that I had more discretionary time available to take on other responsibilities. I reached the conclusion that our talent management process needed to be augmented by a coaching program for leadership so that they could improve the way that they lead their crucial talent. I brought this idea to the boss for approval. For the first few weeks, he kept putting me off as he was too busy with his work to discuss it. I was persistent though and when we finally met, he was frustrated. "Who told you to do this? This program is not important to me," he stated. "By asking me to address this issue, you are taking me away from the important work that I need to do." Since I was proposing a solution that his boss wasn't asking him for, he was inconvenienced and bothered. It wasn't that he thought that this was a bad idea. On an intellectual level, he agreed with the need, and with the solution that I had outlined.

He objected that I was placing him in a position where he had to make a decision. Even though permitting me to proceed was not going to cost him any time or money, to him this decision was agonizing. Allowing it would address an organizational need and would be easy to implement. However, it came with a price. Some senior leader somewhere, possibly even his boss, may ask him why he allowed this to happen without being specifically directed to do it. This boss envisioned a questioning phone call from *his* boss. Perhaps the more senior boss would not have agreed with that action. Nobody was going to ask him about his lack of continuous improvement for the processes for which he was responsible. Therefore, the safe thing, in his mind, was to do nothing. Based upon the way that he was managed by his boss, he was probably right.

This boss didn't even want to discuss what I was doing with my time. He knew that the talent management process was taking less time and energy because the implementation of it was nearly over. His decisions were all about him and his desire to avoid the pain of change. He didn't care about the quality of my work life or the betterment of the organization. This event marked the beginning of the end of my time with this leader. From this point forward, he saw me as the team member who made him feel uncomfortable in his role because I asked something of him that he knew he should do but chose not to do. As soon as the opportunity presented itself, I transferred to another role where I had more opportunities to add value in a job that I would enjoy and work for a good boss.

Both of these bosses in these two examples saw me as connected to the respective changes. In the first example, I was an indirect catalyst for the change because I was the messenger. The message was: If you want me to carry out your change process with the mid-level leaders, you are going to have to change, too. In the second example, I was driving the change of the coaching program because it was needed to fulfill the charter assigned to me.

In both of the examples, these leaders saw change as threatening. In the first one, the boss didn't see the need to change. Perhaps it was because his motivation evaporated with the lost promotion, but maybe even without the promotion in play it would have been difficult for him to change. He was acting under the belief that he was doing the right things, and that change was the right thing "for thee, not me." For me, there was no option but to leave. I could have stayed there and focused on my other duties, however, lots of people could perform these tasks. Eventually, the organization would have figured that out. When my boss perused his morning paper while we met in his office, he told me about my value to his organization.

In the second example, the boss was threatened by a fear of failure. In his self-absorbed world, he could calculate only a downside for himself by agreeing to allow me to implement the change. The organization didn't expect him to be the boss in the traditional sense. Therefore, he didn't care about his duties as a boss, and the organization didn't either. Instead, he was a glorified individual contributor, with people reporting to him. Peers who had joined the team after I did were all in the same position. They were rudderless, with unclear responsibilities, struggling to figure out on their own what they were supposed to do. Not being managed didn't absolve the team members of demonstrating value. The newer team members who were assigned fewer responsibilities were receiving lower performance evaluations, as a consequence of having a boss who avoided making decisions. I could very well face the same fate in the future. At a minimum, I had to live with myself. Why work for this boss, finding ways to make myself look busy, when I could work for somebody else who needed the value that I could produce?

Both of the organizations in the two previous examples hired me to introduce changes while working for bosses who resisted change. These were extreme cases that don't come up every day. Therefore, the third example of this type of bad boss might be more typical. In my HR capacity, I received a call one day from an irate team member who told me that his boss was not confirming to his team members that they could take their yearly vacation until the last minute. Delaying this decision meant that if they were traveling anywhere, their expenses, such as airline fares purchased at the last minute, would be high. Although this boss's action wasn't a violation of company policy, it certainly wasn't a best practice.

The team member was frustrated by this boss's actions and asked if I would talk with him about this, a request to which I consented. Upon sharing the team member's concern with the boss, he informed me that there was a good reason that he didn't want to commit in advance to the vacation plan. He didn't want a support request to come in from a senior leader at a time when too many team members were on vacation and impair his ability to deliver the needed support. By waiting until the last minute to commit, he would have a better picture of the needs at the time. Further discussion yielded the information that this issue of a lack of available resources had actually never happened before. Therefore, it appeared that he was not addressing a problem, rather he was struggling with having to make a decision.

The team member who approached me with the original issue encouraged others to come forward. The inability to decide on when to allow team members to take their vacations was not the only decision that this boss avoided. When team members brought him requests for outside development opportunities, he would sit on them. As with the requests for vacations, this boss didn't want to be caught short-handed. This delay caused some team members to miss the desired opportunity entirely because by the time the boss finally made a decision, the opening closed.

This boss also delayed making decisions on how to resolve disagreements between team members. The more significant the issue, or the more distance between the conflicted parties, the more he delayed a decision. Most of the time, this boss resolved disagreements about the work by doing it himself, thus taking away the source of the conflict. Or, he would side with the team member who was the most strong-willed and against the more accommodating one. This inability to deal with conflict significantly impaired the ability of the team to meet its objectives. Another area that caused this boss to lock down was in the realm of continuous improvement. When team members brought him suggestions that would require a change, as most of these decisions did, he would shelve the issue, pending his "further study." It had gotten to the point that team members stopped bringing him suggestions entirely.

My ability to encourage this boss was limited, especially since, in his mind, he had no reason to change. The team member who brought the original issue to me, seeing that nothing was going to change, wisely decided that he had had enough and moved on, accepting another opportunity. How could this situation have been allowed to continue for the length of time that it did? Perhaps some history is helpful.

This boss was placed in charge of a support group that was known for its stagnant processes. This had not always been the case – there had been a time when this team was taking a leadership role in the support that it was providing to the organization, by introducing new technologies. This team was responsible for advising organizational leaders who were contemplating critical business decisions. However, over the years, this team's performance had been eroded by a string of bad bosses. Organizational leaders believed that this boss would use his technical prowess to introduce new technologies that would invigorate the team and improve its level of support. His leadership ability, or lack thereof, was not taken into consideration before placing him in charge of the team.

What the organization got was a boss who was very highly educated and credentialed, but who was very afraid of making decisions since he didn't want to be wrong. He avoided improving any of the team's processes since he believed that he would have to take a risk and implement changes that the organization might resist. You might think that the organization would not put up with this lack of leadership. However, he remained in the role for much longer than he should have. The senior leader who hired him decided to keep him in the position as he was afraid of removing him, probably due to an inability to admit a mistake. However, I believe that the reason went deeper; he was just as change resistant as this boss was. It goes back to the adage that leaders tend to hire others in their image.

How could bosses like this exist? Since so much of successful management is about change, you would think these individuals would derail before they got too far in their careers. No organization leader would ever say that they would promote a boss that resists change since change is so much of an essential part of the nature of work today. There are three reasons that these bosses exist. First, organizations don't use the right criteria to make boss selections. In the case of the second and third boss examples, these bosses were smart and possessed impressive educational credentials. That's why they were selected. In my experience, organizations use these easy-to-assess criteria when they don't know what is really needed to be successful as a boss.

The second reason that these bosses exist is that they never made the transition from individual contributor to leader. Because they were uncomfortable with leading and maybe didn't know how to, they stuck with the tried and true. They may have thought, "If being a successful individual contributor got me to this point in my career, why not continue leveraging my strengths?" In the case of the second boss, he was not used to having to make decisions that would impact others. It was his prowess as an individual contributor that won him this promotion. Continuing to reward him as an individual contributor, in his role as "boss," does not provide an incentive to change.

The final (and I believe greatest) reason that these bosses exist, is that the organization allowed it because of the way that it expected these individuals to perform. This may at first seem contradictory—I said earlier that no organization would say they want bosses that underperform. And yet, these organizations enabled these dysfunctional bosses to thrive. In the case of the first boss, he was placed in his current role because he was a problem solver, a take control hands-on boss. His history with the organization was one of being moved from one difficult challenge to another, challenges that required someone to take charge and get things done. The same people that were rewarding him for his previous contributions, for his tactical leadership, were telling him that his career was limited because he wasn't strategic enough. If he wanted this promotion, he would have to change. However, was the organization supportive of his development? They left him on his own to improve. They surely didn't wait for him to change before making the promotion decision.

In the case of the bosses in the first two examples, I could have stayed where I was, go through the motions and perform unsatisfying administrative duties. In the case of the first boss, my career stalled, and I certainly wouldn't have grown. In the future, it would be quite possible that some boss would in turn look at my mediocre performance and lack of motivation in a dim light. In the second case, my career was more "safe." Some team members were more motivated by "looking busy" and enjoyed the fact that there were low expectations because the boss was absent and not interested in leading. I could have joined them and watched my skills atrophy over time. But what about the long-term consequences? Would the organization permit a group to exist that added no value? It was a personal choice that I made when I decided to move on in my career and decided that these bosses' leadership styles were unworkable for me.

In the case of the third example, I watched team members work for a boss who made their lives a living hell, in the short term, because he couldn't or wouldn't make needed decisions, decisions that impacted their work life as well as their personal lives. In the long term, they were team members in a support group that was failing in its charter. If they waited a long time to leave this boss, how would that appear on their resume when they finally tried to find a new role? What accomplishments would they be able to point to that would make them worthy candidates in the face of competition from the members of more proactive teams? For those who decided to wait it out and hope that this boss would eventually derail, I leave you with this question: How confident are you that the senior leaders who put these bad bosses into those positions to begin with will wise up and promote a good boss in his place?

The Boss Who Does Not Handle Change Well	
How This Boss Behaves	**The Impact on You**
Refuses to make changes that relate to you meeting your objectives.	By refusing to allow you to fulfill the purpose for which you were placed in this job, your career is in jeopardy. Perhaps this will not be with the boss who made this decision. However, in the future with another boss or with an organizational cut-back, your career will be at risk. Even if those consequences are far in the future, your skills could very well atrophy while you wait.
Procrastinates making decisions on seemingly simple matters, without apparent reason	This could be the tip of the proverbial iceberg. What important decisions is this boss vacillating on that are under the waterline and unseen? These larger decisions will probably have a detrimental impact on your team and ultimately your career.
Resists efforts of continuous performance improvement to your team in the face of increasing organizational demands	In addition to the frustration of a boss who doesn't listen to your helpful suggestions, the reputation of the team will suffer, because there is an increasing delta between how your team performs and what the organization requires. This will have an ultimate impact on how you are perceived by being part of an underperforming team.

Chapter Seven

Does Your Boss Trust You?

Trust is the fuel that drives the engine that is excellent leadership. Without trust, there can be no empowerment or challenging others to take on more responsibility or providing them with a risky development assignment so that they can grow. In my opinion, if you are searching for the simplest definition of great leadership, it is the word "trust." In Chapter Four, I discussed the work of McGregor and his Theory X and Theory Y. The former theory is based on a foundation of a lack of trust, and the latter is based upon trust.

When I talk about trust (or lack thereof), I'm not referring to the isolated person who has violated our trust by not living up to their commitments or who had been dishonest, and we don't trust them as a consequence. I'm referring to a boss who has a belief that all people are inherently untrustworthy, as a default, without knowing anything about them. In the eyes of this boss, anyone who works for him will do the least amount of work possible and get away with as much as they can. People are dull, unimaginative, and self-serving. They only care about their short-term interests and not the larger good of the organization.

Moreover, this boss believes that he is smarter than his subordinates. His promotion to be your boss was because of this. Since he is more intelligent than you, you need direction, control, and micro-management. After all, he has all the knowledge, and he is the only one that can be trusted. What makes this belief so comical is that these leaders who believe that they can't trust their team members were once "untrustworthy" team members themselves. Of course, when they were in this role, they didn't believe that they were untrustworthy or dull or needed direction and control. However, now that these individuals are leading others, they experience a cognitive dissonance between how they view themselves and what they believe about others.

My best example of a boss who fits this description occurred when I was the head of HR for a business unit in a reasonably large organization. Due to an organization change the current head of this business unit, to whom I reported, was replaced by another boss from a different part of the organization. This boss had a reputation as one who could take charge and be depended on to get results. Within a few days of his arrival on the job, I began to understand how he operated.

My peers and I were part of an organization-wide group tasked with evaluating our roles, to ensure proper job grading and the appropriate position on the organization chart. It was a fairly common practice to conduct such an analysis on new roles. This process commenced weeks before the new boss's promotion. When the new boss arrived and learned that this task force was meeting for this purpose, he was angry. Rather than ask me about the task force's charter and my involvement in it, he immediately concluded that my participation was for the nefarious purpose of self-promotion. This behavior is a natural reaction from someone who mistrusts the actions and motivations of others. To him, there was only one reason why someone would participate in such an effort, and that was to increase their pay beyond what it should be, thus cheating the organization. His assistant notified me about his displeasure. When we met, I tried to offer a complete explanation. It didn't seem to matter; he had already made up his mind, to change it could cause him to change his paradigm of mistrust.

I think that part of the reason that the new boss and I were unable to develop a collaborative relationship with was that he did not like the work that I had been doing in the organization. Over the preceding couple of years, I had been working with senior leaders to use data to make quality talent decisions on who would fill future leadership positions rather than rely on gut feeling, which had been the practice in the past. I also was gaining some success in creating a focus on the development of future leaders. One of the best ways to help these individuals gain experience was to provide them with challenging and meaningful development assignments that would involve some risk, such as giving them additional management responsibilities or placing them in charge of operations in trouble. Often an individual in this position wants to know why the organization is giving him such a challenging assignment because if he fails, his career could derail. It is only fair to let him know the positive impact that success would have on his career. It is in the best interest of both the organization and the individual for him to be successful. Being truthful increases the likelihood of success. This transparent behavior also opens the door with the individual to discuss what support he needs to be successful in dealing with this developmental challenge.

This degree of transparency was anathema to this boss. We met to review what I was doing regarding developing leaders to make the right talent decisions and increasing transparency. In about three sentences, he distilled his philosophy of management. He told me that he did not trust any of his direct reports to make decisions as to who the successors in their various organizations were and that he, and he alone, would make those decisions himself, and would not share those decisions with this group. If he did share those decisions, these direct reports would tell the successors that they had made it and that they would no longer need to develop, and they would just sit back and rest on their laurels. Not only did he not trust others around him, but he also didn't trust the conclusions of the tools that the organization employed to assess the capacity of our management, no matter how much evidence there was. The only time that he agreed with this data was if it reached the same conclusion that he had.

This organization had a sizable arsenal of independent assessment data that they had invested in to determine each individuals' strengths and weaknesses against a role of greater leadership responsibility. Following each assessment, a consultant would brief this boss on the results of those in his organization. These consultants went into detail and cited specific examples from where they drew their conclusions, supported by a solid reputation of years of providing accurate data. All of this was to no avail; he chose to pay attention when data matched his own opinion and dismissed it when it didn't match his own.

This boss, in his mind, was the smartest person in the room. He was the chess master, and those that worked for him represented the pawns, knights, and bishops that he would move on the board as he saw fit. Those pawns would perform as he expected them to, or else. Their aspirations and motivations didn't matter, as became evident to me after a discussion that I had with someone who was a successor for a leadership position. I had been asked, by my previous boss, to seek out this team member to understand what his career aspirations were. At the time, he was an individual contributor widely respected for his technical prowess. Therefore, senior leaders thought this respect could translate into excellent leadership when leading highly specialized individuals. This team member told me flat out that he was not interested in being a boss and wanted to spend the rest of his time in this professional role, and he would be delighted if I would pass that on to senior leaders. During our next discussion of successors, which occurred with this new boss, I relayed the team member's comments to him, to no avail. His philosophy was that no matter what the assignment is, this team member will take it and like it. The boss didn't care what this individual's motivations were, and this highly skilled technician remained on the successor list for a leadership position.

During these same discussions of successors, with his direct reports present, this boss let it be known that he would determine who the future leaders would be. What was astounding is that there were 250 positions in question, of which probably 20, on average, would turn over every year. There is no way that any one individual would have all of the right information in which to make the right decision in every case. However, he didn't see that. When you are the smartest person in a room made up of untrustworthy team members who can't be relied on to make as good of a decision, it all makes perfect sense.

I have found that obtaining the opinion of others is essential in diagnosing whether a boss is a "bad boss" that is not worth staying under, or if he is just an "ugly boss" that you can work with (more on ugly bosses in the next section). In this case I sat down with a trusted peer who was in my role in another part of the organization and had worked with this boss previously in a more junior position. I shared how my boss behaved and asked how this squared with his knowledge of his behavior from before. I learned that this boss had pushed his manager to allow him more autonomy in making decisions to select future leaders for the leadership positions in his organization. The very thing that he denied to the management in his new role was something he insisted on when he was in a very similar job. He wanted more autonomy because he felt that he was the best person to make the selection decisions. His new direct reports had been his peers when he was in his previous roles and had similar levels of experience, yet he determined that they couldn't be trusted. He would make the decisions for them. If you think that this sort of thinking doesn't make logical sense, you would be right. However to an individual who doesn't trust others, it makes perfect sense. Such people see themselves as bright, creative, dedicated, and highly skilled. Those that work for them are lazy, unimaginative, unskilled, and self-centered. These bosses don't care about the best interests of the organization, only themselves and the desire to control.

When he didn't have control, this boss pushed for more authority and participation in decision making, based on the argument that he had the most knowledge since he was closer to the work and people that performed it. He argued that he could be trusted to make these decisions. Now that he was in control, his beliefs about people were 180 degrees different. Was he wrong then, or was he wrong now? This dichotomy of beliefs highlights the foundational fallacy in the belief system of the untrusting boss.

This boss changed my most key responsibility away from identifying and developing key talent to one of improving and monitoring HR KPIs. The idea was to hold all bosses accountable for achieving HR objectives. On the face of it, it wasn't a bad idea. However, providing direction was not his real purpose. Instead, he wanted to set up a performance management system so that he could operationalize his philosophy of control. Sitting at his desk and gazing at the dashboard for all KPIs organization-wide, he could flout the conventional wisdom, demonstrating that you can micromanage an organization several layers deep.

I again checked with my peer about his behavior. Was this the way he was in his previous role? According to my peer, this boss had a reputation for controlling others. He was put into his current position because he could be counted on to deliver on results, personally, and not through others. This behavior was consistent with how he managed as he rose in rank. He succeeded by applying new practices so that he could continue to operationalize his untrusting and controlling management philosophy. In his last role, his span of authority had expanded beyond his field of vision. In order to maintain control or the illusion of it, he implemented this KPI process with a digital dashboard on his desk with red and green lights to quickly identify those who were out of compliance. Now that he had risen to an even higher level, he needed to expand it. The critical point here is not what he did, but why. He wasn't interested in driving continuous improvement or motivating others to higher levels of performance by bringing out the best in them. He operationalized his philosophy of mistrust by implementing a system designed to monitor and control others tightly and to punish the miscreant offenders who stepped out of compliance. Sometime later, following the implementation, I heard from organization members that this boss would call sometimes a couple of layers below him to berate them if they were out of compliance, the goal being a punishment, not an improvement.

I chose not to remain under this boss and work in this role. I surely wouldn't be doing him any good, since there where many others who could provide him a better-quality job for what he was looking for in the senior HR role. I would not be happy since the skills that I possessed were not valued. There were other parts of the organization where they would be considered valuable. I certainly wasn't benefiting the organization by serving a boss who I knew to possess the characteristics of a bad boss, and who, at best, would provide this organization mediocre performance. Shortly after he began implementing his KPI process, I determined that it was time to leave, and I accepted a position in another part of the organization. It was clear that this boss didn't want me in his part of the business anyway since he and I had very divergent philosophies on the role of a leader.

This boss's behavior was that of a micromanaging autocrat, one who was motivated by an inherent mistrust of others. It is relatively easy to identify a micromanaging autocrat. It's a different story to try to determine how a boss regards trusting others. In the above case, this boss was very open about his beliefs. He told me in no uncertain terms his opinions about people. Not all bosses are as open about their beliefs. Deciding whether you can work with a micromanaging autocrat can be tricky because not all leaders who behave this way possess this same fundamental belief in the lack of trustworthiness of others. Other motivations drive this behavior, and we'll explore those in a later chapter. However, for now, let's say that just because a boss is a micro-managing autocrat, you may be able to work with him because underlying this behavior, there is a capacity to trust others. The key is to identify those beliefs before you act.

The following example illustrates how to identify these beliefs. I was once asked by my boss to work on an organization-wide task force. The assignment was full time and was estimated to last for a few months. This task force had been working for three months and was perceived to be struggling, as organization leaders expected more output considering how long they had been meeting. My boss asked me to volunteer for this project, as my technical expertise was in alignment with what the task force was addressing. The idea was to help this team to move forward.

I was looking forward to this challenge until I arrived and met with the task force leader and team. In my first meeting with the team boss, I was told in no uncertain terms what my role was in this team and what I would be addressing. He was not interested in my suggestions as to what I should be doing or even my advice as to how to complete the assignments that he gave me, let alone my ideas on fulfilling the team's charter. I was assigned work that was more administrative rather than the work that was more aligned with my technical expertise, which struck me as odd. This individual, placed in charge of this team, did not possess any professional experience. Instead, he was assigned this role because of his leadership experience. Usually, I'm alright with being led by someone who doesn't possess any technical expertise, provided that they "get out of the way" and let me do my job, which was not the case here. Although I was perplexed by his lack of interest in utilizing my expertise, I attributed it to my newness to this assignment. I figured that after a break-in period, I would be able to work on something more value-added.

As I began to interact with the other team members, I discovered that my experience with this leader was not unique. The other team members experienced the same degree of oversight even now, three months after the team started. Since I did not know this leader before this assignment, I decided to do some checking with those that did. I spoke to people who

I respected and who I knew would be candid with me about how this person behaved when he was not leading this task force. When I met with these individuals and described my experience, I found that this autocratic behavior was very much his modus operandi.

Over the next two weeks, I learned more about the projects that the task force was addressing. I was appalled by how sophomoric they were. They were planning on recommending very cosmetic changes without addressing the underlying systemic issues. The conclusions that they were reaching weren't going to be acceptable to senior leaders as they clearly missed the mark when compared to what was outlined for them in their charter. I shared these outputs with trusted peers outside of the team for feedback because I wanted to make sure that my own bias wasn't creeping into this process, and they agreed with me.

I needed to build trust with the leader to be able to have more significant input on the critical task force deliverables. At our next meeting to review the status of my current tasks, I explained that I wanted to make this task force successful, and I made a few specific suggestions. These suggestions would have a minor impact on the current trajectory of the team but would improve the quality of the output. Not only was he not interested in my suggestions, but he also became angered at the attempt. In no uncertain terms, he told me that he didn't care what my expertise was and that he would determine what actions were needed. He was placed in charge of this task force because he knew how to get things done, and senior leaders expected him to deliver.

Over the next couple of weeks, I watched his autocratic behavior with the entire team and listened to how he interacted with others. No matter what actions I took that were in alignment with his direction, there was no change. I was frustrated over my underutilization. I was not adding any value to this task force, either. There were plenty of others who could do what I was doing. Plus, I was deeply concerned about the direction in which this team was heading. I certainly didn't want to be part of a project that was doomed to failure when they presented their findings to senior management. In the end, I went to my regular boss and asked him if I could be removed from the team. I argued that I joined the team believing my expertise was needed but that in reality, it was not. He agreed with me, and within a few days, I was back in my regular job.

In both of these examples, I employed the tactic of obtaining multiple points of data over a period of time to make this bad boss determination. I also used others to reach this conclusion, both in the way that I observed these bosses treat others and by validating my findings with trusted colleagues, asking them if they saw the same behavior as I did.

Bosses who don't trust others impede organizational performance by preventing their people from utilizing their skills, knowledge, and abilities to solve the obstacles that they are being faced with or develop frame-breaking ideas to take performance to the next level. They damage the individual's ability to add value in the future by not preparing them through the lack of challenge or by not involving them in today's critical decisions. In our competitive global environment, if you aren't developing your skills, they are eroding, making you less likely to reach your career objectives.

In the next part of this book, we'll get into the ugly bosses. These are the ones that you can work with, provided that you have the right strategy, and you have the patience to carry it out.

The Untrusting Boss	
How This Boss Behaves	**The Impact on You**
He is the smartest person in the room.	This boss feels that he is the best person to make decisions for issues when you are more qualified, based upon your knowledge and experience. Therefore, you may have to carry out or live with a less than optimal solution, which could negatively affect your performance. Plus, working in an environment where you aren't listened to saps your morale and sense of self-worth.
Assumes guilt unless there is clear evidence to the contrary.	Since your motives are considered suspect, you will have to continually put time and energy in defending your actions, which could be better spent on improving performance.
When mistakes are made, punishment, not prevention, is the order of the day.	The learning that comes from making mistakes isn't automatic. Rather, it comes from feedback and reflection. Because this boss seeks to punish rather than prevent, he increases the likelihood that mistakes will be repeated, thus impairing great performance.
Your ongoing career development is not important, unless it meets his goals.	Your career progression will be out of your hands. This boss will make these assignments based upon his need, not yours. Since your motivations, needs and desires aren't considered, you stand a very good chance of being developed for something that you aren't interested in, or for a job that limits your future career potential.
If he wants your opinion, he will give it to you.	By telling everyone what they are to think and act, the overall performance for the

	organization can't exceed the boss's capacity to perform. This could very will mean mediocre organizational performance. Without being given the freedom to put your motivations and intellect into your job it will be very difficult to learn from it and grow and to increase your capacity to take on new challenges.

Part Three

The Ugly

Chapter Eight

The Political Boss

The political boss is the boss that acts like a politician. Just as a politician's goal is, first and foremost, to be re-elected, the political boss's goal is to get promoted or to gain power. You, the team member, are one of the tools that the political boss can use to achieve his end. In contrast, a good boss utilizes the strengths of his team to accomplish goals that are best for the organization. A good boss has personal goals that would benefit both him and the organization. The political boss's intentions aren't that complicated: they are self-serving. The goals of the organization aren't important.

To achieve his personal goals the political boss elevates the importance of form, which can trump substance depending what he perceives to be the best way to achieve his ends. Political bosses may focus on aspects of the job that have nothing to do with achieving results, such as appearance. I once worked for a boss who made sure he walked in front of the row of senior leader offices just to be seen, even if it meant that he would be going out of his way. Another political boss that I knew was passionately concerned with the way that team members dressed. He included a discussion of what to wear whenever he knew that team members would be meeting with senior management.

Part of the aspect of form that this type of boss focuses on is the cultivation of relationships with key stakeholders. He uses these relationships to develop the political capital needed to reach his career goals. On the face of it, there is nothing wrong with developing relationships with stakeholders. Good bosses will strengthen ties to do what is best for the organization. However, for the political boss, what lies under the waterline of these relationships is the fact that he uses them to achieve his political ends. For example, I once worked for a political boss who loved to ingratiate himself with others so that he could manipulate their thinking to get what he wanted. He wouldn't chance allowing his proposals to stand on their own merit—instead, he hedged his bets by relying on his personality to push them through. One of the problems with this boss was his belief that people are malleable and could be manipulated to serve his purposes.

A further example of this manipulation is the way that the political boss uses participation as a way to develop a relationship with employees. This boss is smart enough to know that he can gain the support of others by involving them in decisions that affect them. However, as a manipulator, he is careful to use participation in a limited fashion as a tool to gain support, but does not box himself in by giving up any control or taking a risk. He is afraid that team members would suggest something wild and impractical where he would have to say no and risk alienating the team. The political boss strikes this careful balance by seeking participation around safe non-controversial topics such as: "how should we accomplish our assigned objectives?" or "how should we improve the working relationship with key stakeholders?" Now, there is nothing wrong with seeking the input of others on those type of issues. However, these are topics that typically won't create controversy. More tricky discussions might result from: "how do we resolve conflict among team members?" or "how do we carry out an unpopular decision by senior leaders?" The political boss might avoid these kinds of topics for fear that they would put him in a position where he might engage in conflict with team members.

The political boss assigns work in a way that is similar to the way that he uses participation. Remember, this boss wants to further his career. The last thing that he wants is news of bad performance from a team member to reach the ears of his boss. Therefore, he wants to make sure that he doesn't assign work that is too challenging and could risk failure. That said, he knows that subordinates feel a connection to the work that is delegated to them, which increases their motivation to want to do a good job. Therefore, this boss tends to strike a balance when delegating work. He assigns the task, but hedges his bets by closely overseeing the delegated task so as not to run the risk of failure, which in turn could create a negative impression with his boss. The usual result of this is that team members get confused about their assignments. There are times when they feel freedom, and other times they feel confined and over-managed by the political boss for no apparent reason. This boss is undoubtedly not going to be open about why he is manipulating his team members. The underlying trigger for intervention in the delegated assignment by the political boss is the attention paid to the issue by more senior management. The more significant this task is in the eyes of senior leaders, the more that the political boss is involved in the delegated assignment.

Assigned work can't correctly be performed without the presence of feedback, and the political boss is not afraid to use this tool. He knows that team members expect it and knows that it can be motivational. Motivated team members will be more responsive to his direction, or in other words, to his manipulation of them. In his mind, tough and harsh feedback, even if it is true, may not be received well. That may damage the relationship of team members to the point that they may not be supportive of him. Therefore, this boss tempers feedback by providing praise at the same time. Let's suppose that the "real tough feedback" that is required is that a team member needs to take more initiative in accomplishing their goals on time. If the feedback is delivered bluntly, it may not be received well. The recipient may become defensive and reject it. The master manipulator that is the political boss can overcome this obstacle by cushioning the real message with adding something positive, sort of giving the medicine with some honey. For example, the feedback that the political boss might give would go like this:

> I like the way that you work with Sally; you are a real team player. Perhaps you could work with Sally on ways to be even more effective at meeting your objectives.

How would you feel after hearing this feedback? Probably, you would think that the boss believes that you are doing a pretty good job. He gave you a suggestion on how to do even better. It may also be a good suggestion. However, it does not reflect the actual state of affairs. This team member may not be inclined to take prompt action to deal with this performance problem since there was just an indirect suggestion of improvement. The boss, through this feedback, is trying to maintain a good relationship and obtain some improvement. It is manipulative; it satisfies his needs, but not those of the team member. He's not being honest about the actual state of affairs by only hinting at the performance deficiency.

The tools that the political boss uses to manipulate team members also extend to the realm of skill development. Good bosses use development as a way to build the capacity of the team members to perform more effectively. This is not a big concern for the political boss. Instead, he sees development opportunities as a way to achieve support and loyalty. He knows that team members want development and tends to treat it as a form of currency, buying the support that he needs. Consequently, he looks for the development opportunities that, in his mind, will engender the most goodwill. For example, this might include sending a subordinate to a high-profile program, the one held in a five-star location and intended for rising stars. This might be one that doesn't place a lot of development demands on the participants, but gives them bragging rights when they return to work.

In essence, the political boss goes part of the way on the journey towards being a good boss by the way that he delegates, involves others in decisions that impact them, and gives needed feedback. However, these behaviors are not effective enough to make him rise to the level of a good boss. For example, although diluted feedback (as in the example that I noted above) is better than no feedback at all, the boss "takes the wrong fork in the road" by the way that he manipulates to achieve his ends. This manipulation comes from a belief that he is smarter than others and that others are gullible and malleable. This in turn tends to lend itself to dealing with team members in a condescending and arrogant way. I had a boss that once displayed this to an extreme. When there were mistakes, he would call the offending team member into his office and ask the obvious question such as: "Do you think that the way that you handled this was a good idea?" That boss demonstrated who was in charge by establishing a parent-child relationship. With someone like this, there is no belief in the ability of people to exceed expectations. This boss doesn't consider that important. Instead, what is essential to this boss is achieving his career goals.

Let's take a look at a specific boss that I worked for to illustrate these beliefs in practice. This boss loved to practice what I call "fake participation." Whenever there was a big decision that was needed, he would bring the "team" together to decide on a course of action. However, he didn't rely upon the synergistic group process to make the best decision. He would "grease the wheel" of creative group thinking through the intervention of his already decided upon course of action. As the smartest person in the room, why let others derail his great thinking by coming up with an alternative?

To carry out this participation ruse, he would hold a one-on-one pre-meeting with a "chosen" team member, where he would discuss what the team was going to do when it got together. In these meetings, he would define the issue that was going to be addressed and engage in a brainstorming session of possible alternatives to move forward. When the team member would happen to identify the same solution that he had, he would compliment their brilliant thinking. Then he would suggest that they bring that idea to the meeting and place it before the rest of the team, never revealing that he has already reached the same conclusion. When the team met, he would conduct business as if the pre-meeting never happened. When the team member would bring up the pre-arranged solution, the boss would treat it as a fait accompli.

One might ask why he went through this process. Wouldn't it have been simpler to be more honest to tell the team what he wanted us to do? There is a lot of work involved in having these pre-meetings. Didn't he think that that the team members were smart enough to know what he was doing? Fellow team members tipped me off of his antics when I joined the group. It was a running joke when he would start a new process to guess which team member he was going to pick to be his "plant." In his mind, he didn't care if we knew what he was really doing because it still served his purposes: he was able to balance motivating the team members through participation and to ensure we were going forward with the "best" solution.

This boss loved pre-meetings with his "customers" as well. Whenever he needed to take something to a group of senior management for approval, he would first meet with them one-on-one. I was part of many of those meetings where he would allow me to "make the pitch." His role was that of "schmoozer." He would always wear a nice suit in an environment where a tie was the norm. He would also expect those that attended the meeting with him to do the same. He wasn't afraid to reprimand someone who was underdressed. He would also open the session with a clever anecdote intended to lighten the mood and make the target susceptible to his proposal because of his dynamic personality. Before the customer meeting, we had to meet ourselves and choreograph the main event. This pre-meeting included who was going to say what and when. This process was repeated for every stakeholder that was involved in the final product.

There is nothing wrong with preparing for a significant proposal, including meeting the stakeholders to avoid a mistake in the final product. However, he intended to manipulate the opinion of the stakeholders through form rather than substance. He was so concerned about the relationship with key stakeholders that he had a standing order that any work leaving the boundaries of his control had to be seen by him—this included memos. Instead of allocating our energy to productive pursuits, we spent it on these endeavors.

Why would you want to work for this boss instead of fleeing to greener pastures? If you had a good boss that you could go to work for, you might. Unfortunately, good bosses aren't very common, and you may not have much choice. Even though the political boss is arrogant, manipulative, and self-centered, you can work with him, if you understand what is important to him. Let's look at his positive characteristics. He involves employees in decisions that impact them, provides feedback, and addresses some critical issues instead of running away from them. This last point is vital. As we discussed in the section on bad bosses, many of them don't want to address critical issues that require action; they display a frustrating cowardice that stands in the way of getting the right things done. They impair our ability to be successful. The political boss's motivations aren't pure since he wants to deal with those critical issues that he can use as leverage to further his career. However, he does deal with them, and sometimes, they are the right ones.

I once remember an upset organization member who came to me seeking help in dealing with their boss, who tended to assign work to this individual only to turn around and over manage the task. This caused him to feel that he was being used and undervalued. He explained that his boss had recently assigned him a problem to solve that had come down the chain of command from a senior leader. When he was awarded the work, this individual was told by his boss that after he put his solution together, he would present it to this leader. The original agreement was that this individual would offer the answer to his boss to obtain approval before submitting it. So far so good. However, after presenting his solution to the boss, the agreement was changed. The boss took over and added his thoughts to a more extensive proposal that he wanted to put forth to the senior leader. In other words, the project would include what the senior leader was looking for, but with something additional that the boss wanted from the senior leader. When it came time for the presentation of the plan, the boss was the centerpiece. The team member played a peripheral part, very much less than he believed to be the case when he assumed this delegated assignment. He further amplified that this was not the first time that this had happened to him, and the boss also did this to some of the other team members as well.

We engaged in a discussion concerning why this happened and what he thought should be the appropriate remedy for his concern. A few things came out of this discussion. First, looking important to senior leadership is this boss's primary motivation. Secondly, this individual was interested in getting ahead himself and wanted exposure to senior leadership so that he could accomplish this goal. He and his political boss had discussed this, too, which made sense since the boss was using this team member's motivation as a way to get this individual to take on extra work. We worked on developing a plan so that both he and the boss could get what they both wanted. The individual went back to the boss and made some suggestions of even more challenging projects that he could take on, ones that would improve team performance and therefore make the boss look good in the eyes of senior leaders. In exchange, he wanted more autonomy in interacting with these same leaders. After our discussion, he met with the boss and offered his proposal, which was accepted. I followed up with a couple of months later, and the plan was still in effect and working well. The idea here is that the political boss, like a good politician, is all for making a "deal" if, in so doing, it will help him to further his career. I'm not suggesting that you go to the political boss and say, "let's make a deal." However, you do need to approach him with the intent of improving the working relationship, and with the deal-making mentality in mind.

Let's take a look at a specific example with the political boss that I've been describing in this chapter, as it emphasizes this point. I came to work for this person as a new team member to the organization and had been given the charter to fix a very broken employee involvement process. The person who had been previously in this role had left the organization, and none of the current team members thought that the system was repairable. When I arrived, the organization's leaders were running out of patience but didn't want to pull the plug on this process because they didn't want to create an employee relations problem, by sending a signal that they didn't care about the opinions of organization members. The spotlight was on my new boss to take decisive corrective action, now.

Shortly after joining the organization, I was able to determine what the exact problem was with the process. There were about 30 of these teams in which organizational members left their respective jobs for one hour per week to attend a team meeting that was led by a fellow team member selected by the group through a process akin to a popularity contest. Organizational leaders were not allowed to attend the team meetings, believing that it would inhibit the creativity of the team. This was the way that my boss's predecessor set it up, and it was never changed. Not only were the leaders not allowed to attend, but they also didn't know what issues the teams were addressing. Some of the teams had been meeting for months and could not agree on a problem to solve.

The teams were allowed to work on projects of their choosing, with no accountability to complete this task within a specific time frame. Many of these projects involved improving creature comforts such as upgrading break areas or huge unworkable issues like strengthening morale. Some employees simply used this as an hour of free time, and organization leaders knew it. Most of the employees wanted to do a good job, but with no leader involvement, which would have translated into support, they couldn't get anything done. Frustration was growing to the point that many team members were talking about quitting the process. Further compounding the sense of irritation, there was a lack of training for those that were leading these teams.

As I began to see the problems with the employee involvement process, I also saw the issues that I've described with my new boss. The critical question to answer in these situations is "how can I get my job done?" In this specific case the issue was to fix this program and obtain my boss's support, which would be needed to implement the needed changes. I also had to ask myself: "Are there any mutual interests shared between the boss and me?" Fortunately, there was good news. I needed leaders involved in the process, and the boss wanted to make a splash with senior management to further his career ambitions. I reasoned that if management saw a benefit in having the process, they would support it, and the boss would get recognized for fixing a problem that needed to be taken care of. This would increase his desired political capital.

The chart below illustrates how I integrated what I needed to do to fulfill my charter of fixing this process and meet the needs of my political boss. The first column listed the final recommendations that I made to the boss to accomplish what I was assigned to do. Indicated in the second column are the benefits to the organization. The third column shows the advantage that the boss would receive, meeting his motivations by the implementation of my recommendations.

My recommendations	Benefits to the organization	Benefits to the boss
Require first-level leaders to lead each team.	Increased team productivity as an experienced leader would lead the team, thereby providing direction to those teams that were floundering, or not working on the right issues.	Since I provided facilitation support to the team and therefore saw what each was doing, I could provide valuable insights as to the strengths and weaknesses of team leaders. This information was useful to the boss because he was responsible for succession planning and could he provide insights to senior leaders that they would not have had previously. High-potential leaders could be placed in charge of teams as a way to develop them.
Although teams would still select the problem to solve, leaders would guide the most significant issues that the team could address.	Teams would work on the right problems that have an impact on organizational performance.	My boss would be able to report out on all of the bottom-line improvements that each team is making to senior leaders, thus showing how his organization's efforts, under his leadership, are adding value to the

		total.
Team leaders would be trained in team problem solving and group dynamics.	Not only would leaders run their team more effectively, but they would also learn skills that could transfer to making them better leaders in general.	Since leadership training fell under the boss's jurisdiction, he would be able to add additional offerings that were supported by organizational leaders, thus completing other objectives and expanding his team's impact on the entire organization.

When there is needed support from the political boss, the analysis that I just outlined is critical. Unlike many other bosses, you can't depend on his support unless you can articulate to him how his power will be the beneficiary of your effort. To be clear, when presenting the benefits to the boss, I didn't articulate them in an obvious way, such as "here is how my proposals are right for you." Instead, I couched them in terms of how it would be good for the team as a whole. He was smart enough to see how it would benefit him.

This boss looks at the potential risk of failure and the potential gain of any effort expended. In his mind, he is thinking, why should I invest my time and energy in an activity that is not going to be a personal gain for me? Once he is convinced by the case you have made, you can move him to act with energy. The benefits should be clear: his power base expands and his credibility increases at the same time, all while meeting the needs of the organization.

The boss and I presented the above recommendations to senior leaders, and they were approved, implemented, and proved to be highly successful. Because of that success, my relationship with this boss changed for the positive, as he became more trusting. He gave me more job freedom where I didn't have to check with him before my contacts with senior leadership, saving me considerable time and aggravation. He also expanded my responsibilities to include other initiatives, which came with the rewards that were attached to them. Of course, it was necessary to reinforce to him how my efforts continued to benefit him to ensure that I maintained his support.

There can be something unsettling about helping this self-serving, manipulative boss to succeed in his career so that you can serve the needs of the organization. There are times when you have to hold your nose while taking action. You can be comforted by the fact that I've seen many of the most self-serving bosses derail at some point in their careers. You could leave this boss if you had a good one to go and work for, but that is not commonly the case. The alternative is to do nothing and wait him out, but that comes with its own risks.

Succeeding with the Political Boss

In order to succeed with the political boss, you will need to align his self-serving objectives with those of the organization. Find the "sweet spot" where his objectives match up with what is best for the organization and the accomplishment of your goals. To determine if your boss is the political boss look for these attributes:

- Focuses on form over substance
- Practices "false" participation
- Overly obsesses on the cultivation of stakeholder relationships
- Delegates responsibility, but withholds the freedom to act
- Delivers indirect corrective feedback
- Uses personal development as a reward, rather than to increase capacity

---

Chapter Nine

The Retired-In-Place Boss

For simplicity's sake, I will refer to the retired-in-place boss as "RIP." This acronym should be easy to remember as it has another meaning not irrelevant to how this boss behaves. I've worked for a few of these bosses in my career and have found them very challenging. Let's start by defining what a RIP is: a boss who has determined that his career is no longer critical. He is now carrying out his job responsibilities with the minimum level of commitment, accomplishing only those expectations that are required to get by. You would think that a boss who lacks a commitment to the job would not last too long in today's fast-paced and competitive environment, but many do, and they flourish. In my experience, either they rely on excellent staff to provide cover for them, or they are in oversimplified jobs they can do in their sleep. Frequently, the RIP works for a micro-managing autocrat who likes to make all of the decisions himself, thereby empowering this boss's *modus operandi*. When his boss is making the decisions and taking the responsibility, it's easy for the RIP to sit back without much effort and lead by the numbers. In other situations, I've seen RIPs work for a boss who has low expectations of him, which enables this boss to use a small portion of all the skills and abilities that he brings to the job. For example, the boss may just expect the RIP to perform the administrative aspects of the job, not wanting him to focus energy on changes or continuous improvement.

I've worked with many leaders over the years who had hard-charging careers, strongly motivated by a desire to climb the organizational ladder, a ladder that gets harder to rise as it gets taller. At some point, we all reach our limit. When you are driven by career progression and you find out that the forward march is over, what then is your motivation for coming to work every day? It can happen that after years of making personal sacrifices for the organization they are informed that there is nowhere left to go. When they retire, they will vacate the chair that they are currently sitting in. Getting this news may not be a problem if there are only a couple of years left, as they can use the time to develop a successor. However, I've seen this happen when there are ten or more years left before the boss is retirement eligible.

Not all of the reasons that bosses become RIPs are work related. Very often, our motivations change as we grow older and encounter life's experiences. Sometimes we face a life-threatening illness or the death of a loved one that causes us to re-examine what is important. When confronted with our mortality, spending more time at the office may not have the attraction that it once did. Although changing the focus of one's life away from a career is perfectly understandable, the impact on the organization can be quite catastrophic, if a leader one day is a micro-managing autocrat and the next day becomes an RIP. I've seen this happen. Team members who had been told what to think are now left with no direction at all. They are forced to make decisions in situations where before they were kept in the dark because the leader used to handle them completely. An organizational paralysis results. Eventually, people start self-directing and making their own decisions, which can be a problem if the RIP is the organization head. With no overall direction, the organization tends to devolve into a feudal state, with each group competing with each other for power.

Although I have worked for a few RIPs in my career, there is one that particularly stood out. I accepted an opportunity to fill a new role that had some challenging responsibilities, which required me to leave my current organization. Because I came from outside, I was unable to glean a lot of information about my new boss apart from the interview process. Since this was a new role there was no incumbent and I would be able to add my "fingerprints" to it and shape the job the way that I thought that it should be. Additionally, the role was matrixed, reporting to the organization head who wanted to implement a change process to improve performance and quality and needed me to provide support. This responsibility would occupy most of my time and energy.

For the balance of the time that I was not supporting the change process, I reported to a boss who, in turn, reported to the organization head. This job had a substantial administrative component to it that required that meticulous and accurate records be continuously maintained. Fortunately, there was a capable staff in place that performed these duties with very little intervention from me. This requirement was so essential that there was an annual audit of these records conducted by organizational headquarters every 18 months. Passing this audit was the most critical part of the job for me, according to my boss. It was so significant that failing the review would be career-ending for me and also my boss. His concern about me focusing on this is understandable and fair. To help ensure that a possible failure would never occur, he would personally conduct inspections of the paperwork, just as the auditors would do. However, even an ambitious schedule of "mock" examinations would require so little time from me personally that it would have been silly if this was all that I focused on. For my boss however, it was the only aspect of my job that seemed to interest him because of the possible impact on him.

This whole effort didn't require much management oversight, and for that my boss was thrilled. It was clear by looking at all of his other direct reports that he preferred to hire good people and turn them loose. However, I think it's important to distinguish between a RIP and a good boss, who also employs good people and gets out of their way. The difference is that the RIP abdicates, rather than empowers. Great leaders provide challenging goals, feedback, productive development, and encourage risk taking; they don't disappear. My boss let me alone so that he could focus on his responsibilities and ensure that he could leave work on time every day and focus on his personal life.

Over the next few months, I developed a good relationship with my new boss. I learned that he was ten years away from retirement but had already decided that this was the end of the career road for him. He was building a beautiful new home in the mountains, and this was where he was going to settle after he retired. It would be a retirement of peaceful seclusion, with the next neighbor some distance away, focusing his time and energy on volunteering for a civic organization that provided the satisfaction for him that he used to gain from work. He told me that he used to be hard charging, putting in a lot of hours, but decided to give that up after the work interfered with his first marriage, which eventually ended in divorce. He was now remarried and was not going to go through that again. He used to get highly upset when things didn't go his way. This had caused a lot of anxiety and probably interfered with his health. Since he decided to forgo worrying about career advancement, he felt liberated. There was no longer a need to take things so seriously.

Over the next few months, we spoke less and less about the job, focusing more on our personal lives. My wife and I got together with him and his wife about once per month outside of work and developed a pretty good relationship. Our weekly updates became more about the upcoming weekend than what was going on in the job. We agreed that I didn't have to keep him updated on the details of what I was doing with regards to the change process. That responsibility belonged more to the organization head to whom I also had a reporting relationship. I was under the impression that all was well, but this was soon to change.

After about one year in the job, the change process support role increased in scope, requiring about 75% of my time. Part of this process was to bring together a mid-level leadership team to take an active role in discussing a strategy to support the overall change process and to develop the tactics required to implement it. Accomplishing this step was necessary because the organization head wanted mid-level leaders to take an active role in this change and not leave it exclusively to senior leadership; this would also increase their ownership of this process. This team selected its leader, and my role was to be the facilitator, where I would give the group advice on how to function more effectively as a team. The team had the freedom to develop its agenda. They were encouraged to make changes within their purview. If they needed approval for something outside of their control, they were to come to the organization head for support.

In the beginning, the team members functioned very well. They were able to work through many issues amongst themselves without relying on the approval of senior management, which was what the organization head intended. He wanted them to be more proactive and to take the initiative in running the business—an admirable goal. One day the team decided to focus on human resource policy issues, which was the domain of the RIP, my boss, as he was the head of HR for this organization. The team was concerned that some policies were constraining empowerment and therefore standing in the way of the implementation of the change process strategy. The group invited a member of HR to the next meeting to understand what possible leeway they would have in changing some of these policies. They didn't want the RIP to attend because they believed him to be very resistant to any proposed changes and that he wouldn't give the team a fair hearing.

The group had previously found the RIP to be opposed to any challenges of his policies. He would not be open to anything that would require him to invest management time and energy. Although I suggested to the team that perhaps it could be a problem to not go directly to the person that could have the most significant impact, I could see their concern. The team thought it best to collect more information and put their case together before they confronted the RIP. The HR staff member attended the next meeting and engaged in an open discussion with the team, answering their questions, and provided them with enough input to form some concrete ideas about a path forward. After another meeting, the team felt that it would be able to go to the RIP with some specific recommendations.

The next morning, the RIP called me into his office. He was extremely angry with me as he received a briefing from the HR staff member who had attended the team meeting. He had previously told me about his explosive temper and how he had used to display it earlier in his career. Now I saw firsthand. Shouting, he asked, "how could you allow this discussion to take place?" He was so angry that he walked out of his own office, leaving me sitting there before I had an opportunity to reply. It was the next day before he had calmed down enough to discuss the situation. Although he was not as angry, he still blamed me for what had happened in the meeting and wasn't receptive to my explanations. Our relationship changed after this and became strictly business rather than collegial and trusting.

Although my boss's reaction was extreme and not particularly constructive to resolving the issue, the deeper problem was that I had unwittingly stumbled on a hot button issue for him. One could argue that I was not wrong in the way that I had acted. The action taken by the team was not my decision and besides, they were only asking questions about policy and not changing it. However, the root of the problem was that I had allowed a change in the way that we conducted our business relationship; it was not fully a boss-subordinate relationship with a proper discussion of expectations. We had stopped talking about what I was doing regarding the change process. I rationalized it by telling myself that the RIP didn't need to know the details about this aspect of my role. After all, he was the boss: it was his job to lead me, not the other way around. I gave him what he asked for and met his expectations of me, as he outlined them. Although that is all true, I was complicit in this relationship change.

After this event, I engaged in some reflection about how I contributed to this event. I learned a valuable lesson about how I would interact with bosses in the future—not just the RIP but any boss. My default position when taking on any assignment is to step up, and in a vacuum, when there is no direction to the contrary, I will tend to act the way that I think best. My style of independence and taking the initiative made it easy for me to go along with the RIP when he didn't want to know the details of my role in supporting the change process. He didn't want to lead, which was fine with me. It was a train wreck waiting to happen, and I didn't see it coming.

I should have kept him updated, even though he had given me explicit direction to work with the organization head. Had my boss known in advance what was going to happen with the group, I could have prevented such unpleasant fallout. The problem was that he wasn't interested in knowing everything that I was doing. How should I know when to tell him what is going on? I decided that in the future, in dealing with a boss, especially one who was hands-off, that I would implement a new tactic. I developed a question that I asked every boss who I worked with, where they gave me autonomy: *In what specific areas of my day-to-day work do you need me to keep you informed*? Before asking the question of the boss, you must think through what the possible answer could be. He may not know how to answer the question without some prompting. In the case of this RIP, when I thought through my discussions with him about what his "hot buttons" might be, I realized that I had some data that said that he was sensitive when it came to challenging his HR policies. To prompt those discussions in future, I developed a question that would stimulate the boss's thinking: *What are the areas that I may get into in the future that you need me to discuss with you first?* I've never liked the saying that you need to manage your boss—it sounds manipulative. The idea here is to help both you and your boss succeed, a real win-win. Even an RIP has some boundaries that, if crossed, will shake him back to his role as the boss.

Once I noticed that the anger had receded entirely a few days later, I sat down with the RIP and had a frank conversation about what had happened, or at least my complicity in it. I suggested that in the future, I would discuss those issues related to the change process that were important to him. We agreed that he needed to be informed about HR issues that the teams were debating as they emerged. By having this discussion with the boss, I was able to restore part of the working relationship—at least enough of it to be productive during the remainder of the time that I worked for this RIP.

When working for RIPs in the future, I engaged my boss in an in-depth discussion of the boundaries. These discussions usually took place over months, since most RIPs don't have a ready list of those boundaries that they can articulate to you. I found that what worked best was a series of questions that I employed to develop a collaborative working relationship. I wanted to know what issues kept him up at night; even an RIP faces these from time to time. I also asked him what areas he focused on versus those he delegated to others, which helped me to understand those things that he needed to keep close and were essential to him versus those that he felt comfortable in letting go.

Another tactic that I used was to observe him in action. For example, when we were in the same meetings, what questions did he ask? When he reached out to me, what issues were important to him? I also looked for cues in my interactions with others. What did they say about the boss? In the team meeting that led up to the incident with the RIP I described above, the team members didn't want the RIP to come to the meeting because he would probably over-react to their questions about HR policy. Had I known that before and had I been paying attention to it, I could have used that information to help set needed boundaries.

I've found that the questions are a little bit more challenging to pull off than the observations, since they may cause a certain degree of discomfort in the RIP. Therefore, you should ask them when you feel that you have established a good rapport, and preface them with a statement like, "the answers to these questions will help me to be more effective."

After establishing those boundaries, I had a clear sense of what the "hot buttons" were. To more thoroughly cement this, I didn't rely on the boss to give me feedback on how well I was staying within the boundaries. I would to check in with him every three months to ensure that there were no issues out there that would create problems later. This action was especially important because of my bias towards independent work, which sometimes creates blinders that interfere with me properly seeing boundaries.

Working for an RIP is a frustrating experience for anyone who needs a boss to be a leader. One day an organization member came to me wanting to talk about his boss, looking for some advice. Specifically, he wanted me to help him to find a new one to work for, as he was fed up with the current one. I was in a role at the time where I was trying to fill open positions around the organization. He knew that and thought that I could help him. The cause of his frustration was an RIP, for whom this individual had worked the past three months. This RIP was widely known in this organization and was nearing the end of a long career. He had been leading a much larger and very prominent function before his current assignment. He was moved into this new role to make room for a much younger high-potential leader. The boss was going to be in this role for the next three years until he reached retirement age, and everybody knew it.

This individual and I engaged in a discussion as to what his boss was doing or not doing that caused him to want to leave and flee to greener pastures. He indicated that his boss didn't want to make any decisions. Instead, he told team members that they should handle issues themselves, even for items that required his input. For example, when it was time to develop yearly goals, he told his team members to put something together and he would approve it. He did so without adding any input from his perspective, simply rubber-stamping what was submitted. The boss also canceled the weekly communication meeting that the team used to coordinate work with each other and learn what was going on organization-wide. He also said that he wouldn't be meeting with team members to conduct career discussions. Instead, he told everyone to submit a list of what training programs they wanted to attend, and he'd sign off on them. This boss was putting his leadership on autopilot, just doing what he was needed to get by and nothing more. To this team member the idea of putting up with this lack of direction for the next three years until the boss retired was untenable; he simply saw his career stalling.

I told him that frankly, I might not be able to help him to change bosses since I didn't believe that the organization would support his reason. However, I would try to help him to overcome his boss's deficiencies. We engaged in a discussion of something that could be done to take action that would be supported by this boss and would help benefit the team and him at the same time. Thinking through this, we determined that the one thing that was important to this boss was work-place safety. This boss had been a champion of safety his entire career and indicated just recently that improvement in this area was needed. The team member had some ideas as to how to effect this. We discussed how he could approach his boss, obtain his buy-in for his ideas, and what support the boss would have to provide to make the proposals a reality.

About a month later, we met again to check on the progress. The boss was pleased with the recommendation and gave the green light to go ahead. He even provided the level of support that was agreed. This individual had noticed a change in his boss; he was still an RIP, but he was more communicative. The boss and the individual were discussing other projects that were interesting and would have a beneficial impact on the organization. This individual had changed his mind about his boss and decided to stay.

I had another run-in with an RIP myself, when I was in a much more senior role than the incident I described earlier in this chapter. I worked for an organization that had gone through a management shake-up after the retirement of the organization's head. My boss became the new head. The job opening was highly competitive, with several senior leaders vying for the role. One of the candidates for this role backfilled the position vacated by my boss. This new boss would very likely spend the remainder of his career in this role, working for someone who had been a peer his entire career.

Very soon after the announcement of the new organization head, it was clear that my new boss had "checked out" and became disengaged. When I met with him, he was courteous and listened to me, but provided no direction. He told me that if I needed to see him about something, to feel free to stop by, but it was clear that he didn't have any expectations of me over and above what I was doing already. He was leaving it up to me to figure out what I needed to do going forward, and if I did nothing in addition to that, he didn't seem to care. I ensured that this was not just my opinion: I backed up my observations by checking with others who knew him before the change and those who also worked with him in the current role. These individuals experienced the same lack of leadership.

Applying the lessons learned from my first RIP, I decided that I needed to ensure that what happened before would not happen again. I asked him about his "hot buttons" per the questions that I indicated earlier. After some thought, he told me that he wanted to know about any actions that I would be taking where I would be asking my peers, his other direct reports, to change what they were doing.

I put this new expectation into practice a short time later, as I was implementing a new HR initiative that would require more effort from my peers. When I reviewed this initiative with the boss and discussed the impact it would have on my peers, I was impressed by the change that I saw in him. Not only was he interested, he gave me some valuable feedback about the project and also about my style. He told me that I should throttle back on the amount of change that I was introducing; I needed to get leaders accustomed to one change before I launched another one. At least on this issue, he became an engaged boss, because I hit one of his hot buttons by asking peers to do something differently. In the future, I noticed a change in this boss. I saw both an increased level of feedback and interest in what I was doing. I still would classify him as an RIP, but maybe more of a RIP-lite. For the remainder of the time that I worked for this boss, we had a pretty good working relationship.

In summary, just because the RIP has decided to move his career to the back seat, it doesn't give you *carte blanche* to set your agenda in the mistaken belief that a leadership vacuum gives you free rein. Even RIPs have boundaries of which you need to be aware. They may not easily articulate them, but you need to uncover them if you are going to be successful.

Key Point for Understanding the RIP
Every RIP has a "hot button" That he probably won't share with you. To identify this ask these questions: • With regard to my current responsibilities: which ones do I need to keep you informed of? • What are the areas that I may get into in the future that you need me to discuss with you?

Chapter Ten

The Technical Boss

One of the most common types of bosses that fall into the ugly category is one who has never made the transition from a technical to a leadership role, which I call the technical boss. Almost all bosses start their career as an individual contributor before performing the work of a leader. If they are proficient enough, they can get recognized by senior leaders and offered the job as a boss, usually in the technical area where they have spent their career. This practice makes some sense because, to have been successful in their professional role, they needed to be smart, driven, and committed to success—these are characteristics that could serve them well in a leadership role. However, as we know, there is a difference in job responsibilities between those of boss and an individual contributor.

Being promoted from an individual contributor to a boss is known as a *job transition*. I use this term because this job change is not a matter of taking on more responsibilities—the responsibilities are different. In other words, you stop doing some things and start doing others. For example, a research scientist who gets promoted to being the boss of other scientists stops doing scientific research and starts doing performance appraisals, goal setting, and hiring. Accepting those differences in responsibility will usually mean the difference between an effective and an ineffective boss. I say usually because there are exceptions, as I will soon illustrate.

For the most part, a boss that does not make that transition, in that they are still fundamentally doing the job of an individual contributor, will be ineffective. They are performing the same work as the individual contributors that report to them, or they are micromanaging tasks to such a point that they might as well be doing the work themselves. In fairness to these bosses, this is a difficult transition. Most new bosses struggle with this change for a while. With the right guidance and a strong desire to take on new responsibilities and get rid of the old ones, most bosses will make this transition. However, there are cases where these bosses don't receive the right guidance. Or aren't motivated to want to manage or both, and as a result, don't make the transition.

It is relatively easy to recognize this boss by how they spend their time and where their energy is. This type of boss will gravitate to the technical issues, even if it's not typically part of the job. They also seem to enjoy spending time on these issues. There is a visible uptick in the level of energy that comes from working problems that are within their comfort zone. This boss, more than likely, got promoted because he was good at these. Conversely, they tend to avoid the tough challenges faced by supervising others as these issues fall outside of their comfort zone. These responsibilities include: letting someone know that they aren't performing to standard, assigning unpopular work, justifying controversial decisions that they have to make, or defending a seemingly lousy decision that is introduced by senior management.

Most everybody works for this boss from time to time in their career. I have found it to be the most common type of ugly boss. However, in my experience, there are two reasons why you might see a preponderance of technical bosses. In professional organizations, often these bosses are selected based on performance review data relevant to the individual contributor role but not that necessarily assesses them against leadership capability. For example, in a sales organization, selling to the customer is the key output that means the difference between success and failure. When it comes time to select the next sales manager, the pool of candidates varies from good to mediocre to lousy salespeople. It is natural to gravitate toward promoting the best salesperson. What signal would you send to the organization if you promote an average performer to be a boss? Surely this individual would suffer from a lack of credibility because of his less-than-stellar track record.

The second and more common reason as to why the technical boss exists is that organizations want them. I have worked with organizations that willfully promote the most technically competent person to be the next boss because they don't trust their workforce to make the right decisions without close oversight by someone who possesses the right technical ability. In these organizations, the boss's role is to carefully watch and micromanage so that they can ensure that team members do what they are supposed to do. They believe their staff will take short cuts or not complete assigned tasks if not closely managed. Closely watching them becomes the order of the day. Besides, according to this philosophy the direct reports aren't smart enough to make decisions themselves. The technical boss is there to step into the breach.

These organizations possess a leadership model based upon mistrust. Not only do these organizations not trust their team members, but they also don't trust the technical boss that manages them. Therefore, they need for the boss of the technical boss to be highly specialized as well so that he can closely monitor what the first-line boss is doing. As you can imagine, the next level of leaders does the same. I've seen organizations where multiple layers of leaders are needed to make the decisions that one team member can make.

The best way to know if you work for a technical boss is by watching and listening to the way that they operate. The work of a leader falls into two categories. First, there is the professional work that the group does. Good bosses provide guidance and coaching to ensure that team members achieve the technical standards that are required to meet their performance expectations and further develop their skills to meet the increased performance expectations that tomorrow will bring. They may also provide technical coaching if they see a team member performing below the standard, with the intent of building this team member's professional capacity so that they can excel without the boss's intervention. The second category of a leader's work is comprised of managerial duties such as hiring, appraising performance, correcting sub-par performance in subordinates, and dealing with a conflict between employees or with outside groups. The technical boss spends his time and energy in the first category of work and avoids the second. However, since I know of no organization that doesn't require boss approval for a performance appraisal, they can't avoid the managerial work altogether. Because technical bosses aren't proficient or aren't motivated by leading others, what you often see is ham-handed attempts to venture into this realm. For example, when it comes to making decisions, I've seen technical bosses act indecisively or make arbitrary decisions that alienate team members. When it comes to appraising performance, they focus on the final rating and avoid engaging in a discussion of the process used to achieve these goals or how to leverage this year's performance to improve next year.

An example of this occurred one time when I was part of a team that had an underperforming member. The team was greatly impacted by this poor performance, as this person provided a necessary service required by all to meet their objectives. The end result was that team members would not be able to hit their performance targets. The good boss described in an earlier chapter would have jumped on this issue by pointing out the deficiency to this poor-performing team member, worked through an improvement plan, demanded improvement, and insisted on regular updates. He would also offer development and coaching if there were a skill gap that caused the underperformance. However, the boss in this example took none of those actions. Instead, he avoided the issue as long as he could until the performance got worse. He complained to the other team members about the problem, but only obliquely addressed it with the team member. He mentioned the issue to him, but did not hold him accountable for improvement, let alone work on an improvement plan. After continual erosion of team performance with no end in sight, the technical boss addressed the problem by seeking additional service resources to bolster that which was supposed to be provided by the sub-par performing team member. This remedy slightly resolved the issue, but still didn't address the underlying cause of the team member's lack of performance. It was only when the unhappy poor-performing team member left the organization, and the technical boss was demoted back to being a team member because of his inability to manage effectively, that the problem began to be resolved—by the boss's successor.

Another example of team dysfunctionality occurred when I worked for a different technical boss. This boss loved to bring the team together to discuss long-term plans. We would spend an entire day in brainstorming sessions, papering the wall with flip chart paper that contained lists of potential strategies and how we could put them into action. The boss loved this exercise; he was creative and energetic and complemented team members for their creative thinking. It was these qualities that got him promoted. However, very little of the team effort came to fruition because he just didn't have the skill to put them into action. To take action would require support from outside the organization, and that that would only come from the boss exercising leadership. He would need to exert influence on his own boss by creating the case for the need for change. My boss would have to remain steadfast in the face of organizational resistance to the strategies that he believed were right. This boss never made the transition from a creative team member to be the initiative-taking boss. This technical boss was simply not up to the task. He rationalized his inaction by saying, "the important thing is that we get together to discuss these issues—I don't care if we ever put them into action." You can imagine the impact of this nonsensical lack of leadership on team performance. Each of these strategy sessions became less and less productive over time and frustration built among the team members.

In a third example, I joined an internal consulting team for a large organization, working for a boss that had once been part of the team that he was now leading. His promotion to lead this team occurred because management liked the technical work that he had been performing, not because he had previous leadership experience. This promotion decision made sense in a way. The organization basically wanted the next boss to be a high-level individual contributor who would personally serve them in meeting their technical needs. They were not concerned about how well he set and executed a strategy for his team or facilitated continuous improvement. This was despite the fact that this team needed real leadership—most organizational leaders continually complained about the team's outdated approach. This boss knew that he could have delegated many of the tasks that he was performing to one of the team members who had the expertise to support these types of requests. However, this technical boss felt that he could depend only on his own proficiency. Others to whom he was delegating to might drop the ball. *Why delegate it to others when you can do it yourself?* is this boss's motto. To be fair, he was only meeting the expectations that were outlined for him by his own boss. He was seen as successful because he met those expectations. While he focused on the team's technical needs, he was able to keep management time and energy at a minimum. He did this by only doing what was required by company policy and no more. For example, the policy stated that every year all employees receive an annual performance review and a rating on established goals. To meet this policy, he asked everyone to develop their performance objectives and submit them to him. At the end of the year, he told us what our performance ratings were. There were no challenging expectations nor developmental feedback, nor was there an overall strategy on which to base these objectives.

Let's take a look at the make-up of our technical bosses. In my experience, there are two types. The first is the boss who doesn't like the role of management and is afraid of stepping into that role. The boss in the first example, who led the team with the underperforming team member, fit into this category. This boss acknowledged the problem. However, for him the only acceptable remedy was to hope that it went away, which indeed happened when the unhappy team member resigned. The downside was that it took a long time for this problem to go away—so long in fact that the team was unable to meet its objectives and the boss was removed from his leadership position because of his inability to handle the problem. I refer to this category as leadership adverse. The other two technical boss examples I gave were the boss who couldn't implement strategy and the boss who ignored the role of management. These fall into the second category: unskilled or unwilling. I grouped these two because the remedy for them is the same, as I will soon outline. Unlike the first category, this technical boss recognizes that the management work needs to get done—it's just not the boss that's going to do it.

In the second example, the boss was unskilled at driving the change that he wanted. I know this because when we discussed the desired strategy that he agreed was needed, he just didn't know how to move forward with the necessary stakeholders. In the third example, the boss simply didn't care about his management responsibilities and was open about it. He openly told me on a few occasions that his primary duties were to serve the needs of his boss and senior leadership; everything else was secondary.

Of these two categories—the fearful leader versus the unskilled/unwilling—the second is much easier to work with because this boss doesn't want to do the leadership stuff or isn't very good at it. At the same time, he knows that it needs to happen, and if you are willing to pick up the slack, you may have some leverage. Therefore, if he trusts you, chances are he will allow you to take over as much of the responsibility as he can safely give up. The first category is much more difficult because of his fear of management responsibilities; he doesn't want you doing it either. He realizes that at some point, he will have to take over for what you are offering to do. For example, in the case of the poor performing team member, I offered to the boss that I could mentor this team member, encouraging him to perform better and offering some suggestions on how to increase performance. The boss rebuked this proposal as possibly putting too much "pressure" on this individual. The technical boss was worried that by highlighting the issue more, it might place him in a position where he would have no choice but to deal with the problem. In his mind, by ignoring it, it might go away or fix itself. I also validated my view with those of trusted fellow team members. They agreed with the actions that I was taking and they, too, had offered the same help to the technical boss, with the same resulting outcome.

Let's examine both of the category two technical bosses and look at ways that we can work with them, beginning with the case where the boss actually wanted to develop a strategy and put it into action (the "unskilled" technical boss). In reviewing what the team created in its brainstorming sessions, I noticed that there were some excellent ideas and also some things we could do ourselves as a team to get the ball rolling, without the approval of senior management. I decided to take this to the boss to test my assumptions, and he agreed with my conclusions. I took the step to offer to take those aspects of the strategy that we just discussed and to put them into action on my own. He agreed, and we discussed the next steps and how I would communicate back to him on my progress. I also provided some advice on how he might inform his boss on what we were doing in a way that seemed relatively easy to pull off, even for his low skill level. In a sense, I gave him some tips on how to introduce change, at the same time that I outlined my proposal.

The point here is that I took the initiative to "lead" the process instead of waiting for him to develop the skills and begin to do his job of leading the implementation of the new strategy. Frankly, he displayed so much concern about confronting senior management that he probably would never pull off the task even if he developed those skills. Waiting for him would have been fruitless. The team would have suffered because the strategy, which made good sense, would have gone nowhere. It wasn't a perfect solution, because most of the plan was left undone. However, we were at least able to move forward. We jointly developed an action plan where both of us took some action.

When working with the other category two technical bosses, who do not manage (the "unwilling"), you need to step into the breach and become the neo-boss by volunteering to take the action that this boss won't. This is different from the "unskilled" technical boss that we've just discussed because, in that example, the boss was interested in taking on the strategy, but confidence or competence got it the way. However, in this case the boss doesn't care if the task gets completed or not. The result is the same: if you don't do it, it won't get done. There is a note of caution here. You must engage in this step only after you have had a conversation with the boss after which you are 100% sure that the boss understands what you are doing and is committed to you taking action. If that commitment does not exist, you could be setting yourself up for trouble. Remember, we are dealing with someone who isn't interested in the role of managing. His polite acquiescence today could turn into opposition tomorrow if he gets surprised by a querying phone call from senior management. Even with his initial commitment, ongoing communication with this technical boss about your progress helps you determine if that commitment is wavering.

Let's take a look at an example of how you could accomplish improving the relationship with this technical boss. Our team was receiving feedback from our internal customers, to whom we were supporting, that we were missing the mark in one of our service areas. The boss was aware of this feedback. Still, since this issue would require collaboration with his peers to bring about a solution, and an action plan that would require him to assign work responsibility and follow up to ensure completion, he chose not to address it. In other words, it would necessitate him leading, something that he did not want to waste his time doing. In any case, his boss wasn't asking for it, and any effort here would take him away from addressing the technical issues that his boss was focused on.

I met with the boss and provided a reasonably simple solution and specific action plan that included testing the solution with essential customers before implementation. This suggestion seemed to make sense, and the risk of failure was low, so he told me to go ahead, with the proviso that he hear the results of the feedback from customers before going further. I had frequent discussions with the boss, updating him on the progress of this initiative. I even invited him to meetings that I had with others so that he could observe the progress firsthand. I also highlighted the benefits for him in the eyes of our customers. As it turned out, customers saw it as the right solution, and the implementation worked well. The boss received accolades from his boss, and he was able to focus on the technical issues that he loved so much.

Both of these efforts paid off with these bosses. That said, neither would grow out of being technical bosses for the entire time that I worked for them. The boss in the second example never learned how to turn a good idea into an actionable plan, and the boss in the third example continued to view his role as that of a highly paid individual contributor. However, our relationship was improved as I was considered more of a trusted advisor. I also think this helped me in the realm of receiving higher performance ratings. But even more than that, I was able to gain job satisfaction because I was working on something valuable to the organization as I was addressing issues that improved our team's performance. Therefore, I saw my interventions as a win for both of these bosses and me.

We now return to the boss in the first category, the technical boss that is afraid of the role of management. For our purposes, this boss is in a no man's land between the bad and ugly boss. I say this because you really can't work with this boss the way that I suggested with the other two (the unskilled and unwilling/uninterested). However, I don't think that the situation is as dire as it is with a bad boss, in other words you may not need to leave. Instead, keep your head down, do your job the best you can and hope for the best. Working with this boss will require a considerable amount of relationship building and patience. Chances are, after some time, this boss will have failed, and the problem will have eliminated itself.

In addition to my own personal experience working for technical bosses, I have also helped others with this challenge. To give one further example: one day two team members came to my office, together, to talk about their boss. These two were part of a very technical team, staffed with bright and highly skilled individuals. The team had been in the job for about one year, following the boss's promotion out of it. This boss, as described by these two, was a technical boss, who loved to focus on the professional work of the team and was not very proficient on the leadership side of his responsibilities, tending to avoid them if he possibly could. It was this latter area that was of the most concern to these two.

Notably, they described their team as a collection of highly qualified but opinionated professionals, who did not always agree on the right path forward when they hit an obstacle. Team members did generally get along with each other. However, there were times when a tough problem would present itself that did not have a clear solution, sending everybody to their respective "corners" to battle it out. When they couldn't reach an agreement among themselves, they would take the issue to the boss to make a decision. Here is where things broke down. Each individual who had a stake in the verdict would take the issue to the boss, make their case, and usually, the boss would agree with that person. Then, upon hearing that decision, a different team member, not liking the outcome, would take his solution to the boss, who would end up reversing his previous decision and siding with the new person. This boss was being swayed by the last voice he heard and changing prior agreements. It sounded to me like this was a boss who was afraid to say no.

The two team members wanted me to take their problem to the boss and get him to change the way that he led the team. Although a change in the boss's behavior would be the best solution, I would probably have a limited chance of success. Instead, I asked them if they and their peers would be willing to work issues that needed boss approval out among themselves, and then take the final solution to the boss to obtain his buy-in. I gave them a book on team problem-solving techniques and even offered to facilitate one of their sessions to help them get started. They agreed to give it a try and were able to put it into practice successfully. I followed up with them about one month later, and they reported that although the boss hadn't changed how he led the team, the members at least were able to get around this technical boss's lack of skill, by coming to their own agreements successfully.

In summary, the technical boss is the most common of the ugly bosses. Provided that this boss isn't interested in managing or isn't skilled at it, you could develop a good working relationship with him provided that you are prepared to step up and "fill the breach" and assume some of the management responsibilities. If, on the other hand, the technical boss is afraid of the onerous obligations that every boss faces, then this could be a problem. If the issue relates to tough responsibilities such as managing conflict, confronting poor performance, or defending a controversial position and he refuses your help, then this is probably a situation where your efforts to improve the working relationship will come to no avail. In this case, waiting him out is perhaps the best way to go.

Type of Technical Boss	What to Do When Working with Him
Leadership Adverse	You could try to offer help. However, you will probably determine that the best thing to do is to "duck and cover;" go about your business the best you can and wait him out.
Unskilled	Work with him to put together action plans, go with him to meet with critical stakeholders, continue to offer help.
Unwilling	"Step into the breach" and offer suggestions on what leadership tasks that you can take over. Constantly keep him informed as to the actions you are taking as to ensure that there are no surprises.

Chapter Eleven

The Autocratic Boss

The autocratic boss is one who micro-manages the work of his subordinates. This boss doesn't trust the ability of his team members to perform their jobs without the direction that he provides. The thoughts, feelings, concerns, and motivations of subordinates are inconsequential. When it comes to providing direction, poor performers and excellent performers are seen in the same light and all receive the same direction. While good bosses maintain the right blend of "telling behavior" and "listening behavior," autocratic bosses do not worry about maintaining such a balance. Instead, they tend to be very open about what they think, because they feel it is essential and relevant to share. "If I want your opinion, I'll give it to you," is the autocratic boss's view of establishing a good rapport.

When it relates to your performance, the autocratic boss tends to be candid about what was not done well and less so about what you did well. You got paid for doing your job, what more do you need? He'll let you know when there is a problem, so no news is good news. When giving feedback, this boss very seldom has a developmental focus. Good bosses, on the other hand, will use feedback as a way to help you grow and be more productive in the long term, as in the example of my first good boss when I was fifteen years old. Remember, that good boss pointed out my sub-par performance and told me of bigger and better things that could result if my performance improved. With an autocratic boss however, feedback rarely goes beyond merely pointing out the deficiency. The autocratic boss tends to be good at saying the *"what,"* *"how,"* and *"when."* Taking the time to tell team members the *"why"* is a waste of valuable time. Following instructions and getting the job done his way is everything.

In my own experience, I have found that the autocratic boss is not the worst of the "ugly" bosses. He does have some strengths that are needed to allow you to perform optimally, such as giving prompt feedback and establishing expectations. You may not like his abrupt style and lack of caring for your feelings. However, these are preferable to the tendencies of the technical boss or the RIP boss, who may leave you in the dark, all too often setting you up for trouble as I indicated in earlier chapters. Something is comforting about knowing where you stand.

You are probably thinking about now that this sounds very much like the untrusting micromanaging autocrat boss that we discussed in Chapter Seven, and you are right. There are similarities in the way that these two bosses behave. They are somewhat difficult to tell apart, at least on the surface. The real difference lies underneath in their value system; in the way that they look at people. The boss described in chapter seven is incapable of trusting team members. Doing so would conflict with what he believes to be "true" about people: employees will take advantage of you or take short cuts or lay down on the job if you don't control their actions. Besides, why should you trust subordinates to do the right thing? He knows what is best because he is smarter and more highly skilled than his subordinates; that's why he is the boss.

The "ugly" autocratic boss is different in his underlying set of beliefs than the untrusting boss, in that he is capable of trusting team members. He doesn't, as a default, mistrust others. The bottom line is that to work with the autocratic boss you need to establish trust to have a meaningful working relationship. That is more easily said than done. If both of these bosses are similar in the way that they operate, then how exactly are you supposed to find out which is capable of trusting and which one is not?

To answer this question, let's start with understanding of why the autocratic boss behaves the way that he does. There are many legitimate reasons as to why you see autocratic behavior. It's not uncommon for an inexperienced boss to behave this way, especially if he is highly technically skilled in the area he is now supervising. He merely is sticking with something that he is comfortable with: making technical decisions. The other part of his job, the leadership of people, is messy, and for the neophyte boss it can be a daunting task. He may not mean to be autocratic, but he knows that he can tell people what to do since he used to be good at their jobs himself. He has not yet developed the skills of delegation, developing people, resolving conflict, and having difficult conversations that would allow him to rise above the technical level.

Another reason that a boss may be autocratic is that his boss expects it; he may have an untrusting boss. The last thing that the untrusting boss wants is a subordinate boss empowering his team members. He will give the orders to you and will expect you to convey that order to your team members. He probably has created the expectation that he, the untrusting boss, and he alone will make the critical decisions. If you remember, in my previous example of an untrusting boss, he took the decision-making power for promoting new bosses out of the hands of his subordinates because he didn't trust them. In so doing, the untrusting boss is a position to ensure that these new bosses are the ones who are going to respond most positively to his autocratic micro-managing style by taking orders and in turn demanding compliance from others.

In my experience, one of the most common remedies that organizations take for a weak performing team is to remove the boss. Then the new boss steps in and begins to be an autocratic boss because the assumption is that the group is at fault for the performance problem. This situation is another reason why I see autocratic bosses develop. The boss may have a preponderance of new employees to manage or face inner-group conflict that interferes with the team fulfilling its mission. He therefore has decided, rightly or wrongly, that he can't trust the team and needs to take a firmer hand. This may be even though he is normally trusting.

What you need to do is to diagnose the boss and determine whether this untrusting behavior is part of his nature, as was the case of the boss in chapter seven, or whether it stems from conditions in his environment. The untrusting boss in Chapter Seven made the diagnosis easy since he told me that he was untrusting. His openness about his value system made my decision-making process about leaving him easy. I determined early on that he was not the type of boss for whom I wanted to work. Therefore in your case, it would be best to engage the autocratic boss in a conversation that will help you to determine what his beliefs are. Naturally, this will require some thought, planning, a fair amount of patience, and of course, some risk. To be successful, you need to approach this effort honestly and with openness, with the intent of developing a good working relationship with this boss moving forward.

The best strategy is to start small in this diagnosis as opposed to confronting him about his value system right off the mark. One way to do this would be to engage him in a discussion about the assigned work. Specifically, you can ask him about the degree of freedom that you have to operate in those tasks that he has entrusted to you. Ideally, you should want the most amount of freedom to work, taking into account your capabilities. A good boss would be eager to grant as much freedom to operate as possible, provided that you are skilled in accomplishing this work and motivated to succeed. If that boss wants to maintain tight control and limit your degrees of freedom, then you can engage with him as to why he doesn't want to give you more autonomy. If the answer to this question is inside of self, such as, "that's the way that I want it done," then the boss may be our untrusting friend from Chapter Seven. If, on the other hand, the answer is outside of self, such as "my boss wants it done that way" or "the way that I want it done is a proven best practice," then the boss could fall into one of the autocratic "ugly" boss categories. However, more study is necessary. As I pointed out earlier, never base your diagnosis on a single point of data.

The best way to collect more data is to continue to offer help, suggestions, and opportunities to expand your freedom around assigned work. The response to these suggestions and offers will help to give you the data that you are looking for to determine whether the autocratic behavior is internally or externally driven. The risk of alienating the boss through your entreaties is pretty low since most people don't get offended when you offer help. If your efforts are continually rebuked over time, especially if you are delivering on assigned tasks and meeting expectations, then you could be working for the untrusting boss.

As a way to exemplify this point, I was stopped in the hall one day by a team member who was upset with his new boss. This boss had been a team member until recently, promoted after the removal of the previous boss who failed to perform. This new boss was highly experienced and respected in his field by both the team members and senior leaders. Because of the previous boss's failure, the team was way behind in meeting their objectives. This meant there was a lot of pressure on this new boss, in addition to the normal stress that accompanies learning the job of leading others. Feeling this pressure, the boss turned into an immediate autocrat, forgetting the fact that he had good working relationships with team members, transforming from Dr. Jekyll to Mr. Hyde. By the time the team member came to me, the boss had already squandered a lot of goodwill from his former team members.

We discussed the actions that the boss was taking. Even though he was forcing them down the throats of the team members, were they the right things to do? The team member informed me that he agreed with the actions, for the most part. The solutions were okay, but he and the team members had some better ideas. Unfortunately, they didn't feel that the boss would listen to them. Plus, they felt alienated by the manner of implementation of his plans, as he wasn't consulting with the team members in solving problems that impacted them. It was clear that this new boss was losing the support of the very people that would be able to help him to succeed.

The two of us engaged in a discussion about next steps. This individual felt comfortable with directly confronting his boss with an offer to help him to be successful in his new role—if only the boss would let him. The tough part for this team member was planning how to confront in a supportive and convincing way. We talked through how to have one of those conversations where it comes down to closing the office door and saying, "we need to talk." This team member needed to come to such a discussion armed with concrete suggestions on how he could positively contribute to what the boss needed to accomplish to be successful. Encouraging other team members to do the same might help this situation.

We got back together again a couple of weeks later, and he informed me that the boss responded very positively to the support. The boss felt that he was alone in his struggle to improve performance. He had assumed that it was his job to solve problems, by himself, as this was what he believed that a boss does. When the team member offered the help, it was gladly accepted. Over time this boss included the team members in more of his decision making. Eventually there was a restoration of the working relationship between all of them.

To give another example of an autocratic boss, while I was in an HR role a team member approached me desiring to file a harassment complaint against his boss. I was familiar with the general situation that this individual was facing. He was a member of a team that had recently received a new boss. The old boss was removed six weeks earlier after a relatively brief and torrid stint. The removed boss had been placed in the job because he was bright and highly technical, but he didn't really want to lead. Senior leaders had coaxed him into taking on the assignment by emphasizing the perks and downplaying the challenges of leadership. He had been told things like, "leading others is not that difficult—just follow the procedures, and you'll be fine," and was instructed to just keep focusing on the technical output of the team. His brief tenure proved to be a disaster from the beginning. Terrible conflicts brewed up between team members and productivity dropped. This boss lacked both the skills and the motivation to handle them.

Senior leaders kept him in the role longer than they should have, hoping that he would improve. However, after they reached the end of their patience, he was removed, and a younger high-potential leader took his place. This new boss wanted to prove to senior leaders that he was tough and could quickly turn things around. He came on the scene with guns blazing and within two weeks removed some of the team members who were a source of the conflict. I believe this was meant to be a warning to others who would transgress. He put the other team members on notice that he expected compliance with new goals that he established for everyone, throwing out the old ones.

This team had gone from having no direction to being led by someone who was overbearing. The old boss let the team members define their own goals and objectives. The new one disdained any input from the team on establishing these same goals. This boss even told the team that he would be closely monitoring when they were away from their desks to ensure that they weren't sloughing off in the break room. This incident was the trigger for me to become aware of this situation, as team members began complaining to me that this boss's behavior was demeaning. The way that this boss behaved was somewhat understandable as there were performance problems in the team that required attention. However, he treated all team members the same, assuming all were guilty. Up to this point in his career, in his few leadership positions, this boss did not seem to be untrusting. His actions in this situation were somewhat out of character for him. I believed that the reason behind his change was that he wanted to create an image of toughness that he thought would appeal to senior leadership. It was well known that toughness was a quality that senior leaders looked for when making decisions about future bosses.

Now, six weeks into his experience with his new boss, this team member came to me with his complaint. He claimed it wasn't just his complaint as all of the old team members, who were still part of the team, agreed about this new boss's behavior. We had a lengthy discussion about what had happened and why. At the end of it, the team member, although still feeling aggrieved, could understand that this boss was somewhat justified in some of the actions that he took. We then engaged in a discussion of what we could do going forward, and he backed off on his original desire to file a harassment complaint, for now. The idea would be to offer unsolicited help to this boss for something valuable that would demonstrate that if he were less autocratic and more participative, he would reach his own goals more effectively. In other words, put this boss in a position where he would be asking himself, "I wonder what else these team members could offer if I only asked, instead of directed?"

After brainstorming some ideas, we came up with the idea that the team member could offer to act as a coach for new team members to help them to get up to speed quickly. He believed that this would be important to the boss since he had neither the expertise nor the time to do this sufficiently. Such action would also be a win for the team member because the longer the period of time that these new employees spent trying to learn to be effective, the longer he would have to carry their load. He could contribute to cutting down this time. We also discussed briefing team members on how they could use similar methods to help the new boss to succeed. Over the next few weeks, I checked back with the team member on the progress. The new boss had responded positively to the team members' entreaties to help. With each one of them, he became less autocratic and more participative and behaved more as he had in previous roles.

Another example of a situation that I encountered could illustrate an excellent way to improve the working relationship with the autocratic boss. A new boss had just been assigned to lead our team. The reason for the leadership change was that the previous boss was underperforming. The performance problem was not limited to our team alone; it permeated the entire organization. Competitors had eaten away at this organization's market share, and profits had been declining. This mature organization was struggling to survive since it hadn't made many of the marketplace changes that its more nimble competitors had taken on. Senior leaders were in a state of panic as to how to address this issue. When all else fails, blame it on the workforce! "You people aren't working hard enough, and you need to pick up the pace" was the order of the day, as opposed to addressing the real problem. What was required was reinvestment in the core competencies that made this organization great and utilizing recent technological advancements. However, such a step would require capital that the organization didn't want to invest. It's much cheaper to push your employees to work harder.

As a result of this situation, team members now had greatly expanded job responsibilities without having been provided any additional resources to meet those objectives. The duties were ones that required a different skill set; one that team members lacked. On the positive side, senior management took advantage of this crisis to remove underperforming management, hence our new boss. This new boss was very experienced, having served in management positions in other parts of the organization, although leading a smaller team. It was clear that the organization didn't want to take a chance on a first-time boss by promoting somebody out of the team. They were looking for someone who they knew would be committed to improving performance, and this new boss didn't disappoint. I didn't consider him a first-time boss (a subject which will be discussed in the next chapter) since he had experience with managing others in this organization and the same technical area.

In the first meeting with this boss, the team got the pep talk that was very much analogous to the locker-room half-time talk that a coach would give to a football team that was down by two touchdowns. The dialog was one way, with him telling us how we were going to improve and that our livelihood depended on this improvement. He ended his diatribe with the obligatory inquiry, "does anybody have any questions?" Upon hearing none, he informed us that he was going to meet with each person one-on-one to review their goals and activities. The stunned team walked out feeling dejected since many were doing their job just like they were supposed to. They felt like scapegoats for a poor organization strategy.

The next day I had my meeting with this boss to review my goals, which was the first time that we had ever had a face-to-face meeting. We spent little time on the pleasantries of getting to know each other, rather he started by re-hashing his speech from the day before. To me, the meeting felt very much like an interrogation. His questions centered on how I spent my time and there was not one question about how I thought performance could be improved. It was like he didn't believe that my opinion mattered. I walked out of the meeting with the understanding that I would improve performance by taking on additional responsibilities. However, there was little discussion about *how* I could be successful in taking on these responsibilities, only that I had to do it and that I'd better be successful at it. Other team members who had their meetings with him said the same thing about their interactions. This boss did a lot of preaching and seemed devoid of answers as to how exactly he wanted us to achieve these new goals of expanded responsibility, only that he expected top performance.

Perhaps this boss was at a loss as to how to achieve these goals, just as we were. I believed that he saw the organization's performance problems as lying mainly outside of the team's hands. The view that there were strategic and organizational reasons for the poor performance was widely shared, except by the most senior management. Following his initial application of the "stick" in terms of threats and intimidation, came the use of the "carrot," which came in the form of tee shirts with slogans and team lunches, with speeches, designed to rally the troops. You could tell that the boss did not have much faith in these remedies; he was simply going through the motions. He read the script but didn't believe in the hype. Highly excited employees, if one could get excited by such ploys, weren't going to resolve the systemic failings that caused the organizational problems in the first place.

Over the next few weeks, the organization's troubles increased. There was a senior management shake-up, with some of the old tenured leaders replaced by younger leaders, who hopefully had a few new answers. The only solution seemed to be cutbacks, which precipitated a round of layoffs, which was followed by resignations by some of the organization's most noted performers, who possessed industry recognition. These were the very same people that the organization needed to retain in these troubled times. Team members were struggling to take on new responsibilities. Morale was sagging, and turnover was increasing as some team members were leaving, saying that their new responsibilities fell outside of their skillset and career motivation.

Soon after this new boss arrived, I began to enquire about his leadership behavior, as I had no first-hand knowledge. I talked to individuals who did know him, and their assessment based upon their relationship was very different than the autocratic behavior that he was exhibiting now. Others who worked for him in the past found him a boss who listened and involved others, very different than the boss that was now leading this team.

Over the next few weeks, I engaged in some trust-building measures designed to improve the working relationship with this boss. For example, I openly discussed my struggles with taking on these new responsibilities and sought feedback from him on my efforts. Also, even though he didn't ask, I offered suggestions on the support that team members would need to handle these additional responsibilities.

One month into my relationship with this boss, I decided to take this working relationship to the next level. During our weekly update meeting, after he finished his questions of me and our meeting was winding down, I told him that I understood this business situation had to be hard on him, as our boss. I told him that I knew that he was trying to improve our performance in a callous business environment. He seemed to appreciate my empathy and opened up about his frustration about the situation, telling me that he realized that everybody was trying to do their best and that almost all of the problem was organizational and not with the team. He opened up a little about his concern about the recent resignations of key people and was worried about other team members leaving. I suggested that he speak with everybody directly about this and listen to their concerns, to which he agreed.

The discussion marked a fundamental change in our relationship, for the positive. I demonstrated to this boss that I wanted to do an excellent job for the organization. I also displayed empathy for this individual's seemingly untenable position, that of making changes that he knew weren't the right ones. He tried to do the right thing to generate performance improvement without the tools to make such improvement since so many of the organizational problems were out of his hands.

In future interactions with him, which increased, he would share his concerns and frustrations, and I would respond empathetically. He increasingly sought my opinion, was open to my suggestions, and showed appreciation for my efforts. Other team members, who did the same, noticed a difference in his behavior as well. It was clear that this boss's autocratic behavior was not his default style. This behavior had been prescribed to him by the organization, which told him to be tough. This had come at the expense of enlisting the support of the very people needed to turn things around, which could have been achieved by providing developmental feedback and a display of empathy with what team members were going through in assuming these new responsibilities. Or it would have been constructive to seek the opinions of team members on how to carry out assigned work. Those actions would have been productive and those of a good boss.

This boss couldn't change the structure of the job; he had no choice about the job responsibilities that the team members now had to assume. Senior leaders wanted him to autocratically hold team members accountable for this change, not to accept any excuses and to demand compliance and results. This boss knew that this was not the right way to reverse the organization's sagging performance. He decided to take a chance and display the type of "good boss" behaviors that I just described because deep down, he was not a bad boss. His value system and belief about the power of human creativity and ingenuity emerged because that was true to who he really was.

What made the difference in my working relationship with him was my focus on wanting to fulfill the expectations that he outlined for me. I displayed a concern for the position that he was in, made suggestions on what was needed by the organization to accomplish these goals and showed my desire to help the entire team, not just myself. This last point was significant since this was something for which the boss was responsible. It goes back to the idea that if you focus on what is important to the boss, it is much easier to build a great working relationship with him.

The real critical first step to working with this type of boss is to determine if indeed this is an autocratic boss or the untrusting boss described earlier. Knowing the difference between the two is complicated since the behavior displayed by these bosses can be very similar. It takes time and patience to diagnosis what is behind this behavior to determine whether a value system of mistrust drives this boss. This chart may help you in making that determination.

Behavior	Untrusting Boss	Autocratic Boss
How this boss uses his intellect	He assumes that he is the smartest person in the room and values his own opinion over all others, discouraging or even punishing free-thinking in others.	Won't solicit the opinions/ideas of others at least until the development of a good working relationship, but when offered a suggestion, there could be a positive response.
How this boss addresses questionable behavior in others	He assumes that there was nefarious/self-serving intent on behalf of	May very well ask to understand what happened and why, before passing

	the others, assuming guilt.	judgment.
How this boss addresses errors that others commit	Punishment is the remedy for the offender.	Some attention paid to understand why the error happened with steps taken on preventing a reoccurrence.
How this boss views the career/development of others	The boss decides what's best for you; your goals/motivations are superfluous.	There will be some recognition that you have goals and motivations, considering them.

I want to make one caveat on the first point in the above chart on how the untrusting boss uses his intellect. Every bad boss that I've worked for had at least one person working for them that had a particular niche skill that was both important to this boss and that he lacked. Because of this, he treated those individuals very differently than others on the team. In these cases, the bad bosses were respectful to the opinions of these individuals and provided them with much more latitude and freedom to operate than anyone else. They did this because even a person who believes he is the smartest person in the room realizes that there are some things that he cannot do. For example, I once had a bad boss who determined that he critically needed someone close to him that was good at a particular technology. He certainly didn't want to take the time to learn this skill, nor take the time away from his regular job to engage in this task, so he found somebody who could.

Also, in the table, I indicated how these bosses react to questionable behavior and errors made by others. Let me elaborate on this. There are times when we all take actions that cause questions as to why we chose this course, the motivation behind it not being immediately known. Ideally, we would want others to understand why we did something before passing judgment.

When it comes to your career and development, the mistrusting boss doesn't care about your goals and motivations, he is the chess master, and you are the pawn. With the autocratic boss, he at least recognizes that they exist. If you behave in a trustworthy way, offer helpful suggestions, take responsibility for team success as well as his success you will go a long way in transforming him from an autocrat to a better boss.

Building an Effective Working Relationship with Your Autocratic Boss

- Keep focused on your assigned work, no matter how difficult.
- Share areas of concern with your boss and seek his feedback to remedy them.
- Offer suggestions on how to deal with the performance problems that are driving this boss's autocratic behavior.
- Empathize with his circumstances and offer help to him to reach his goals.

Chapter Twelve

The First-Time Boss

This chapter is different than any other in this book. Some bosses are good, some are bad and others, ugly. However, every boss is a first-time boss, once. For our purposes, the first-time boss is the boss promoted into a permanent boss position for the first time or an experienced boss placed in a new setting for the first time. Settings could include joining a new organization from the outside or taking over a new function from inside an organization in an area in which the boss has no experience, such as moving from managing a sales function to managing R&D.

The first-time boss is very different than any other boss that I've discussed in this book in another way, too. This category of boss is not about a management style necessarily, as is the case with the political or autocratic boss. Instead, it is more of a starting position until we know more about this boss. Knowledge will be gleaned as this boss experiences the new role. This boss may not know himself what kind of boss he is until he spends time in the position. His management style may be change as a result of his self-confidence, the direction of his boss, or because of organizational culture.

I've worked for some pretty good first-time bosses and also some that have been pretty bad. The reason for this broad spectrum from good to bad has to deal with the variables confronting first-time bosses. These may include how much training they receive before they move into the role. Another one is how much support they receive after their promotion. Do they understand the basics of what it takes to manage? Do they have a more senior boss who takes them under their wing and helps them along? I have seen some bosses who just get thrown to the wolves, so to speak, without any support. It's almost as if the organization doesn't think that the job of leading others is challenging and that anybody can do it—usually because they over-value the technical side of management. I have seen other organizations prefer the sink or swim method. They prefer this Darwinian approach—survival of the fittest—because they see their people as expendable commodities. They think that if this person doesn't work out as the boss, we'll simply get rid of him and put somebody else in the role. After all, there are plenty of others that could be selected to replace him.

Another variable that determines the effectiveness of the first-time boss is the relationship that he has with his new employees. Very often, when organizations are looking to promote a boss to lead a team, they promote the brightest person out of that team. Now this boss is leading former peers. There could be petty jealousies that create problems, such as resentment from team members because someone else was promoted instead of them, causing a desire to see the new boss fail. I have seen this especially as a problem in organizations that have promotional processes that are somewhat arbitrary, such as choosing someone to be the boss because he has the most educational credentials and not necessarily because of his past performance. Or it might be that the new boss received his promotion because he was the best at building a good relationship with organizational leaders.

A third variable that impacts boss effectiveness is the condition of the team when the new boss takes over. Perhaps the previous boss was terrible and had to be replaced because he poorly managed the group, leaving a trail of destruction in his wake. These problems could include infighting between team members that were given competing responsibilities, or that the team has a damaged relationship with its customers, causing a loss of credibility. In my experience, a group that is under the leadership of a bad boss experiences a lot of turnover. Since this turnover usually involves losing the most experienced and best-performing team members, the group now faces the problem of trying to accomplish its mission with new team members who aren't yet up to the task. Therefore, the first-timer may step into a situation where he needs to learn to be a boss and deal with this dysfunction at the same time.

You may think that it is crazy to put a first-time boss into the situation that I have just described. However, in organizations that place a boss's technical ability above his ability to lead others, this action seems to make perfect sense. The paradigm dictates that the ideal remedy for a team that is not delivering is to drop in a technical boss who can make up for all the team's performance shortcomings. If that boss doesn't work out, then he will be swapped out for a new one with stronger technical ability. These organizations deserve the performance problems that they have created. If they would take a step back and see that it was poor leadership and not a lack of technical ability that caused the failure, then they could possibly avoid the continued performance problems. In my experience, when I've seen a team fail to accomplish its mission, 80% of the time, you can tack it up to poor leadership, either because of an ineffective boss or systemic organization problems created by senior leaders.

The first-time boss's motivation for taking the job is another variable that can impact his effectiveness. I have seen many times when senior leaders are looking to promote the most technical team member, and they sell him a bill of goods by downplaying the people management side of the role and playing up the need for placing someone in the position with strong technical ability. In the team member's mind, since he really wants to be in a technical job and earn a boss's salary and benefits, why not accept the promotion? Or, his motivation may be that he truly wanted to make the transition to leading others and took the job with his eyes wide open. He may have desired to make the career move to stop being a technician and start being a great boss as described in the first part of this book. The assessment of which of these scenarios apply is critical since it may well determine how you will work with your new boss. If it is the former, and he isn't interested in managing and wants to continue to be a technician that happens to be in charge, your tactics will probably be different than if his motivation is the latter and he wants to be a good boss. We discussed in previous chapters how to deal with this boss. It's a simple matter of diagnosing which ugly boss it is and applying the right remedy.

What is essential for you in this situation is to get to know the new boss enough so that you understand what motivates him. Specifically, why did he take this job? What support is he getting from his boss? What is the relationship between him and his boss? Finding this out may seem like a daunting task. After all, you are the team member and he is the boss. There is a definite power differential and asking these direct questions may not be advisable. It all depends on your relationship with this person.

I believe that the eyes are a powerful tool in observing how your boss behaves. Remember the old axiom *actions speak louder than words*. How does your boss spend his time? Does he try to do the work of the team himself, or does he manage others who are doing it? If he spends time doing the work himself, then that may indicate that he is moving in the direction of being a technical boss. How does he interact with his direct reports? Is he aloof, or does he try to develop a working relationship with you and your fellow team members? Remaining aloof could signal trouble. It could mean that he doesn't trust others, or he is not confident in his abilities to lead and doesn't want to show it. Or, he isn't receiving organizational support through coaching from his boss or HR on how to succeed in his new role. He may be reluctant to take any action for fear of making a mistake.

When you meet with the new boss, what questions does he ask you? What information does he share with you? That is, of course, if you meet with him at all. If he avoids directly meeting with you or your fellow team members, that could be highly significant. Ideally, you want to see a good dose of "telling" behavior such as sharing information about the company and providing feedback along with "seeking" behavior such as asking you for input on important decisions and obstacles that you face in accomplishing your work. If, for example, he tends to make decisions himself when he knows that you have critical information that would add to the decision quality, that could mean that he is trending towards being an autocrat. If this boss avoids making decisions, it could mean that he is trending to being a technical boss, or perhaps he doesn't want to manage at all, like the RIP.

The critical point is that you need to diagnose before you decide on a course of action and that diagnosis can be accomplished, in large part, by watching and listening. I suggest that developing a good working relationship with the new boss is more critical than with any other boss. Developing this relationship could be difficult for you if this new boss was previously a peer, promoted instead of you. If you are harboring any negative feelings as a consequence, it's essential to get past them. This boss is going through many stressful changes. He is learning about the team, working with a new boss, and leading for the first time. These changes can naturally cause a great deal of stress. Helping this boss to work through these changes will pay dividends for both of you in terms of a stronger working relationship.

However, I would like to add a caveat regarding the new boss. It's probably no surprise to know that new bosses have a higher failure rate than experienced ones. You want to avoid a situation where you've decided that you can't work for this new boss, leave for greener pastures; only to find out that the new boss got fired. Therefore, you need to consider what your organization's tolerance is for new bosses who aren't successful. As I indicated earlier, I've seen organizations use a Darwinian approach to selecting new bosses: "If this boss doesn't work out, then we'll just discard him and put somebody new in his place," even to the point of outplacing him. I've seen situations where, six months previously, an individual had been a rising star because of his technical ability and was placed in a boss role where he failed miserably. Now, he is unemployed. If this is the type of organization that you work for, then you may want to wait it out and see what happens. Such a way of dealing with talent is callous and self-defeating. Many such organizations take a high performing individual contributor and test this individual's potential to take on more responsibility, by promoting him to a boss role without the proper preparation. Organizations that treat their key talent this way deserve the problems that they create.

As someone who has done a lot of coaching over the years, one of my favorite coaching engagements is called transitional coaching. This type of coaching is where I work with a boss who has taken over a new role. I work to help him to think through how he is going to be successful in that new role and what are his plans on handling critical issues. For example, we discuss topics such as how he is going to connect with key stakeholders. Or, how is he going to understand the strengths and weaknesses of his team? Typically these types of engagements last for 100 days after the individual starts his new job. A great example of this involved a new boss hired by my organization. Senior management wanted to hire someone with excellent technical experience and educational credentials as the boss for a team that needed to ratchet up its mediocre performance. Senior management's theory was that such a boss would introduce new frame-breaking technology that would cause this group's performance to soar. To find such a boss, senior leaders decided that they were willing to compromise on the job candidate's demonstration of leadership ability. After a pretty exhaustive search, they hired such an individual. His leadership experience was fairly minimal, consisting of leading ad hoc project teams.

When this new boss started, we began working together to help him to transition into this new role. The output of our first few meetings was an action plan that he was committed to undertaking. As one might expect, some of the actions consisted of specific steps that he was going to take in developing the relationships with key stakeholders such as his boss, peers, and team members. Part of this process, one month in, was to check with stakeholders to see how he was doing in implementing the agreed actions. Usually, the one coached collects such feedback. However, he felt very uncomfortable with doing this and asked if I would manage this feedback for him, which I did. When meeting with the team members, I could see why he was a little uncomfortable in collecting it himself. The team members all said the new boss did have an initial meeting with them and was pleasant enough in the way he communicated, however, by and large, they found him very aloof. He tended to hang out in his office with the door closed. When he went through the work area, he very rarely had anything to say. When he communicated, he tended to use email rather than face people directly. One team member told me the boss would walk past someone's desk and into his office and send them an email, when it would have been more natural and more effective to stop and tell them directly. This behavior raised concerns for the team members because they were uncertain about the future, knowing that some changes were coming. The team knew that the new boss was hired to introduce new changes and to shake things up. His lack of communication only served to raise the level of anxiety. In the absence of information, people tend to fear the worse.

I shared this feedback with the boss, who agreed with it all. He went on to say that he was, by nature, rather shy and struggled with developing the type of collaborative relationships that he needed to gain commitment from his team. We talked about times when he was more comfortable being cooperative with others. It would have been rather difficult for this individual to be as successful as he had been in his career if he acted this way all the time. This boss indicated that he was most collaborative when he knew that he needed support from others for implementing initiatives that are important to him. In his new role some processes were severely broken, which impaired the ability of the team to achieve expected results. He had some concrete ideas on what was needed. However, since he was new to the organization and the way that things were done, and didn't know the people that he would need to connect with to make things happen, he went into lockdown. His natural aloofness and tendency to shy away from others took over.

Our discussion then turned to how he could get started on what was needed to overcome his aloof ways and connect with the team members to move his agenda forward. He focused on starting slow in discussing this with the team, sharing it with each one individually, starting with the person with whom he felt the most comfortable. I followed up with him two weeks later, which was the allotted time for him to reach out to each of the team members. He told me that not only did he speak with each person individually, but he also brought the group together to go further into the subject. During these sessions, team members made suggestions on his ideas and provided the right organization guidance on how to get the whole project completed. This process seemed to break the ice, and from that point on, the working relationship between boss and team improved.

Not all first-time bosses receive the benefit of a coach to help them through. So, how do you break the ice with a first-time boss who is aloof like the one we just discussed? I have found that there are some excellent questions to ask, whose answers could form the basis of a productive working relationship. They could also assist the boss in being successful by helping him think through what priorities should require his focus.

- What are the key initiatives that you would like us/me to focus on over the 90 days?

- How do you plan to communicate your expectations or convey important information to me/us?
- How would you like me/us to communicate with you?
- What should I/we do differently in working with our key customers/stakeholders?
- What do you plan to do differently from your predecessor as it relates to me/us?

As you can see, these questions can be asked by you individually or as part of the entire team. These should get you up and running with the new boss in the short term. Later, after about one month, you can ask about longer term initiatives. Ideally, when you have a new boss, if he is a good one he will start communicating the answers to these questions to you within the first few days. However, if nothing happens within the first two weeks, it is a good idea to get together with your peers and discuss a strategy to go to the boss with them. If you don't feel that you're going to get the support from peers, there is nothing wrong with taking them to the boss by yourself.

Let's take a look at an example to illustrate how I worked with a new boss. In a previous chapter titled "The Political Boss," I described my work on improving a team process. Shortly after I was able to develop an excellent trusting working relationship with that boss, there was an organization change, and my function now reported to a new boss. I knew this boss somewhat since he and I had worked together to make the teams in his part of the organization more successful. There were two interesting aspects of placing the new boss in this particularly exciting role. First, this boss did not have the technical ability in the function that he was now leading. He came from another function entirely and possessed no knowledge of what was required to be successful in my area other than the experience that he acquired from me when I was helping his team to be successful. Secondly, the head of the organization was mentoring this boss. It was also known, through my interactions with this organization head, that he intended to place more value on the team process, making it part of a broader strategy to improve overall performance in his organization. Operationalizing this strategy was the primary responsibility of my new boss. The head considered him as a rising star; he was placed in this role to round out his skills to prepare him for bigger and better things in the future. This leadership change and the intended actions of the organization head made perfect sense.

I gave my new boss a couple of weeks to get settled into his new role before I ramped up my relationship activities with him. I used this time to get more acquainted with his expectations and to answer his questions about the work that I was doing. I also took the time to talk to trusted peers who had more of a knowledge about how he operated as a boss. I found out that he was a strong technical leader who relied on his expertise to successfully manage. This analysis matched up with the intelligence that I had received that the head wanted to get him out of his comfort zone to see how he could manage in a function where he had no technical expertise.

In the third week, after I started working with him, during one of our weekly update meetings, I asked him a question: How can I help you to be successful? This question may seem strange because most people think that it's the job of the boss to make his team members successful, and it is. However, if I want to have a trusting relationship with this boss, then I need to establish a win-win relationship. I also need something as well. You can't have a win-win without meeting your needs as well. I needed the freedom to operate. I sure didn't want someone with very little knowledge about what I was doing to be telling me how to do my job. I also wanted a boss who would care about the problems that I encountered in making this team effort successful, which required more senior-level support.

Let's think about what is going through his mind and his needs in this scenario. He doesn't know much about my job except at a superficial level. I don't really need a lot of direction anyway. I can be of service to the organization by giving this boss the skill rounding that he needs to prepare him to take on greater responsibility. It's essential to think through what you think his answer to the question is going to be. I knew that this team process was vital to the head, as it was something that he was touting as a way to improve organizational performance, and this new boss was his hand-picked high potential. I felt that my boss's response to this question would be around taking these teams to the next level of performance.

His response to my question was very candid, and he appreciated the ease in which he could bring out his concerns. He wanted to gain more of an understanding of what it takes to make the team process effective as part of his ongoing education. Some teams were better than others; why is that the case? He realized that a lot came down to the way that each boss supported the teams in his area. How can we increase that level of support? We decided that he would shadow me when I facilitated the team meetings and when I met with bosses about what was needed to make their teams more productive, and when I delivered training to the team leaders.

Over the next couple of months during this shadowing process, he asked thought-provoking questions with the intent to learn. When we had our weekly meetings, I asked him if this shadowing process was working for him and if there was anything else that I should do to help him. These actions led to a win-win relationship. In our efforts to make these teams more effective, he was learning about this process as well. This boss used the "power of his office" to reinforce to obstinate managers, who didn't see the team process as necessary, the need to be supportive. Everybody knew that the distance from his mouth to the organization head's ear was very short. Therefore, I had obtained more senior management support for making this process, for which I was responsible, more successful. Hence it was a win-win.

In summary, the boss in this example had leadership experience, although he was new to the technical area that he was now leading. I've worked with other first-time bosses who were experienced in the professional field but new to leadership. In either case, the process of developing that collaborative relationship is the same. I suggest that the first-time boss is the most difficult ugly boss to work with because the way that he leads is unknown, perhaps even to him. In the case of the boss in the last example, he had a track record of being direct and somewhat autocratic. When he took over as my boss, he became much more questioning and observant, recognizing that he was slightly out of his depth. If I had employed my relationship-building strategy based on his previous leadership style, I would not have been successful. I needed to give him time in this current role to see how he would lead.

In the case of the boss who has never managed before, his style may change as he gets his feet on the ground and discovers who he is. The way that he leads may also be impacted by what his boss expects of him and the organizational culture. First-time bosses are usually reluctant to stand up to a boss that has different expectations of the way that they lead. Therefore, collecting data is more critical with this boss than any other. If you feel that you haven't received enough information to form a diagnosis, then you probably haven't collected enough data. Displaying patience is critical with this boss, as he goes through this transformational learning period. Your offers of support will go a long way towards building a collaborative working relationship.

Building an Effective Working Relationship with the First-Time Boss

- Diagnose the circumstances behind this boss taking this job and his support structure, as this will impact your strategy.
- Work to understand his expectations of you. Don't wait for his direction.
- Ask him how you can make him successful.
- Jointly develop an action plan. Implement the plan to make him successful.
- Plan check-ins with him to ensure that the plan is hitting the target.

Chapter Thirteen

The Mercurial Boss

I once worked for a boss who managed a mission-critical support team in a very sizable organization. The customers for this support group were the organizations' senior management. The boss was receiving feedback that our team had not been providing the quality level of support that it should, that many senior leaders weren't happy about this degradation of performance, and that the reputation of the team had suffered in recent years as a result. The boss brought the team together and said that we were going to reverse this condition and regain our reputation. As a number of us, including the boss, were new to the team, we had no real insights about the cause of this problem. At least nobody said that they did.

As a way to remedy the problem, the boss asked all team members to engage in an exhaustive study that began with interviewing each of the key stakeholders, which was a relatively large group of individuals. Following this interview process, we were to prepare specific solutions and an implementation plan. All involved team members, including myself, spent the better part of a month on this issue. After this process, we sat down with the boss and shared the data, our solution, and the plan to remedy the condition, as instructed. The cause of the problem, as illuminated by each of the stakeholders, was that our team was not proactive in confronting senior leaders to get them to do their jobs. In other words, we weren't enforcing our practices, and senior leaders wanted us to be stricter with them and hold them accountable for doing what they were supposed to do.

Upon hearing everything from us, the boss agreed with our analysis, conclusions, and implementation plan. In fact, he was not surprised by any part of what we shared with him. What was surprising to us, however, was the fact that he then decided that this was no longer a priority and shelved the whole project. He announced that it was not the right time because there were other priorities that we needed to address. There was a great deal of frustration and anger on the part of the team members. We had spent considerable time and effort on this challenge only to hear that it was no longer a priority to him.

What I have just described is an example of what I call the mercurial boss, where the boss will change his mind as to his expectations of others or work assigned to them. He does it abruptly and for no apparent reason, almost like some form of attention deficit disorder. These sudden reversals can create havoc and be destructive to both performance and morale. From my own experience, I've identified two primary causes for this mercurial behavior. First, I've noticed that bosses often behave this way when a leadership vacuum exists from above. In other words, senior management is not displaying any direction or worse inconsistent direction, and as a result the boss is somewhat wandering around in the dark. This boss may try different initiatives to see if he can get some type of positive reinforcement from senior leadership. When he doesn't receive it, he drops it in favor of something else. I coached a boss once who had just taken over a team from an ineffective boss. This new boss determined that several changes were necessary because the team was underperforming against its goals. However, these changes were frequently over-ridden by more senior leaders who were change adverse. At the same time, this same senior leadership didn't want to take a stand and provide direction. They left it up to this now frustrated boss to figure out what to do, deciding to veto changes that they didn't like, frequently after having initially given him tentative approval to go ahead. The bottom line was that he was a victim of indecisive senior leadership that wanted him to cure the "disease" of the underperformance of the team, but who couldn't agree to the "cure" to remedy it. When I started working with this boss, he expressed frustration over the starting and stopping nature of the changes that he was making and the impact that this had on the team. As it turned out when we worked together, he had somewhat of a "fire-aim" leadership style, which, when combined with indecisive senior leadership, created a slightly toxic environment. We talked about building relationships with senior leadership to understand their hot buttons and boundaries. Once he started engaging senior leaders more before "firing," he was able to resolve this problem significantly and turned things around.

The second cause of this condition is where the boss himself lacks confidence in his ability to commit to taking an action that he knows is required. The example with which I started this chapter is an example of this. As it turned out, this boss understood the root of the concern that our "customers" had right from the beginning. Assigning the work to us bought him some time. Perhaps he hoped that we would come back to him and recommend that we couldn't solve this problem. It was his lack of confidence in his abilities to deal with this issue that impeded his success. He could have started out by deciding that we weren't going to deal with the problem at all to begin with, which would have been the honest approach. However, that would create awkwardness for him because he would have to explain why. It felt much easier for him to say—after we identified the problem—that this was too difficult of a task to take on when we had so many other challenges. It is difficult to get senior leaders who are more powerful than you to do their job. This gives the mercurial boss an "out" if he wants to exercise it. So, he may take recommendations under advisement and give the matter a "pocket veto," hoping that it will just go away and that we'll be so busy that we will forget about it.

As you can imagine, the path forward is very different depending on the cause of the mercurial behavior. If it is the first, then you need to help this boss to work through the challenge of obtaining clear direction from senior leaders. I once worked under a boss who called me into his office one day and told me that he needed to analyze a problem, including some benchmark research and a recommendation of how to address it. This request seemed somewhat strange as it came out of nowhere, but I complied. At our next weekly meeting, upon updating the boss on this initiative, which had taken the majority of my time during the preceding week, he told me to drop the issue and assigned me a different task that would require a similar amount of time and effort as the first one. I took this in stride—after all priorities do change from time to time. About three days into this project, the boss called me into his office and ordered another change in direction, dropping the current project and moving on yet again to something else. In the last three weeks, I had done almost nothing concerning my regular work. Now these assignments were canceled and new ones assigned. The behavior that this boss was displaying was not entirely new. He would order a direction change from time to time as a matter of course, for no apparent reason. It was annoying, but I had learned to live with it. Recently however, this mercurial behavior had increased dramatically to the point where it moved from being a nuisance to a state where I could not do my job effectively.

I decided that I needed to take action. I sat down with the boss and outlined to him that I was having difficulty accomplishing my assignments due to the other work that he asked me to take on. Not only did this additional work interfere with my regular job duties, but none of it had been accomplished due to the start and stop nature of these extra assignments. I asked him if there was anything that I could do to give him both what he needed from these additional assignments as well as perform my other work. By taking this approach, I offered to give him what he needed and not complain about what I was assigned, even though it was disruptive. If I had focused on the disruptive nature of the assignments, I would be telling the boss that they weren't legitimate. I had no way of knowing if they were or not. Perhaps these assignments were the right things to work on, and he couldn't share the rationale behind it with me.

The boss opened up to me about the cause of his mercurial behavior. He had just recently started working for a new boss, who had a lot of good ideas but was really out of his element. I knew of the new boss, and the scuttlebutt was that he was a rising star who was moving very quickly because of his keen intellect and creativity. This senior leader was coming up with quite a few half-baked ideas and plopping them on the table without any clear direction or even a discussion as to whether or not they were practical. Although these weren't specific assignments, my boss took the initiative and decided to put them into action, as he was desirous of pleasing his new boss. He thought through what he thought his boss wanted and then made the assignment to me to take these vague suggestions and turn them into specific initiatives that would improve performance. When my boss reviewed how his team was operationalizing these half-baked ideas with this senior leader, the leader began to see impracticalities or simply lost interest in them and moved on to chasing the next shiny object. My boss simply adjusted to the new idea and gave out the new assignment to his team.

The mercurial boss wanted to please his own boss, who didn't know what he was doing. Instead, this senior leader was falling back on what had made him successful, his creativity and intellect, using that as a way to generate some value. The idea here was that for me to succeed, I needed to make my boss successful in the eyes of his boss. My boss wanted to help this senior leader to get his agenda implemented, as raw as it was. Specifically, to take his vague suggestions and turn them into tangible workable initiatives. Not surprisingly, my boss was just as frustrated as I was.

I initiated a discussion with my boss on how we might be able to prevent some of the wasted time that we were incurring. Jointly, we developed a plan where the boss would take a few of the team members to meet with the senior leader during his "idea" sessions. The purpose of this would be to think through what would be involved in implementing these wild ideas and hopefully stop them early before we put much time into them. The mercurial boss met with the senior leader, who loved the idea of bringing team members to these sessions. The senior leader enjoyed these creative gatherings as he felt it was his way of adding value. This remedy addressed the problem. By the time the team received a new idea from one of these sessions, it was fleshed out enough to turn it into a viable initiative. The number of started and stopped initiatives was greatly reduced as a result, and my boss throttled back his mercurial behavior.

Earlier in this chapter we discussed the second reason for a mercurial boss: a lack of confidence. As a coach, I worked with an individual that was a perfect example of this second type of mercurial boss. A senior leader once asked me if I would administer 360-degree feedback to one of his subordinate bosses. The senior leader informed me that there were some real concerns with the way that this boss was leading his team, whose performance was lacking. Additionally, team members were complaining to the senior leader about this boss's inability to get things done. This senior leader told me that he had provided this boss with feedback about the issue and that things needed to change. However, nothing had happened so far. He wanted to use this 360 feedback as part of a plan to ratchet up the heat that he was placing on this boss to change. Outplacement was in the offing if things didn't improve.

I discussed this with the boss, who would be the subject of the feedback, and he was open to the process, especially since his own boss placed so much importance on it. Once the feedback was collected and processed, I met with the subject boss and reviewed his results. Two themes emerged from the input. First, the senior leader was not happy with this boss over his inability to get things done. The performance of this boss's team was below par, and issues that were impacting its performance were left unresolved, just as this senior leader had told me in our initial meeting. The second issue was that the team members who reported to this boss reported a lot of mercurial behavior in that he had started and stopped several initiatives, causing frustration. During the review of the feedback, the boss acknowledged both issues, agreeing with the feedback that he received. He told me that these two issues were linked.

Fortunately, the feedback report listed some concrete projects that the boss had initiated that were examples of the team's disappointment with his lack of leadership. The boss designed each of these projects to address the performance problems that his team was facing. We discussed these to understand the reason that the projects had been stopped. As we unpacked the events surrounding each of these projects, two things became apparent. First, he thought that each of them was the right solution to deal with performance problems. Second, each of the implementations moved forward until he met an obstacle. When he met resistance either from senior leaders or from peers or his team members, he melted, and the implementation ceased, and the project was dropped. Specifically, he decided that rather than try to persist and overcome the resistance, it was much easier to stop try something else, hence the mercurial behavior. As he explained, in each case the project was the right thing to do and he had a good plan for implementation. However, what did these plans in was his lack of confidence in his abilities to overcome the resistance. He simply didn't believe in himself. For the first time, he looked in the mirror and acknowledged that he was letting himself down by not pursuing what deep down inside, he knew was the right course of action. Armed with this knowledge and the realization that if he didn't make some changes, his career with this organization was in jeopardy, we worked on some techniques that would help him to overcome resistance. As he employed them, we talked through how he was doing. Over time, he gained enough confidence in his abilities to overcome opposition and to be successful.

What if you are a team member who reports to this boss—how do you identify and resolve this behavior? In this case, the boss's mercurial behavior centered around his lack of confidence in dealing with resistance from others on what he wanted to do. Look to see if there is a common cause of the mercurial behavior, such as an inability to be strategic, resolve conflict in others, or difficulty in dealing with resistance. Once you have identified that common theme, then you should step in and offer to help to handle those issues. Sticking with the above example, you could ask your boss if you could help him resolve this resistance. If the resistance is from your peers, you could help the boss convince others of the value of what he wants to do. If the opposition is from the boss's peers, you could go with the boss to meet with the resisters to overcome their concerns. If it is a conflict between others, perhaps you could offer to help him mediate. If the inability to be strategic is the concern, you could provide support in working with him to develop a strategy.

Another strategy would be to wait out the mercurial boss. In the example that I illustrated with the boss who could not deal with resistance, he would probably be eventually replaced if he didn't change his behavior. However, what would be the cost of dealing with more of his behavior in the meantime? Taking action on your part could mean an improvement in the working relationship with your boss. That is an investment that could very well pay future dividends.

Building an Effective Working Relationship with the Mercurial Boss

- Diagnose the true cause of the mercurial behavior (i.e. dealing with resistance or being strategic)
- Jointly develop and action plan and follow up.

Part Four

More Good Bosses and Fewer Bad Ones

Chapter Fourteen

What Do Organizations Need to Do to Ensure Good Bosses?

Starting with the work of Douglas McGregor on Theory X and Theory Y, over the past 60 years there have been countless books and studies on the subject of leadership and the impact on performance. Organizations are quite happy to spend billions of dollars on leadership development programs to the tune of $14 billion a year, according to a 2014 study by McKinsey[v]. Why do we still have so many organizational leaders that give this area lip service, but simply don't care what the research says? In Chapter Four, I gave reasons why bad bosses exist. In my opinion, the most egregious reason is that many organizations don't actually want leaders that display the characteristics of a good boss. In too many cases, those characteristics are antithetical to the value system that these organizational leaders possess. As a result, they are impervious to what this vast body of evidence says about what great bosses can do for their organizations. To protect that value system, these types of leaders are willing to implement management control systems that ensure, at best, mediocre performance. Therefore, I don't think that we will run out of bad or ugly bosses. Let's look at what can be accomplished to at least reduce the supply of them and increase the number of good bosses.

As an individual employee who has to thrive in the environment that bad bosses create, there isn't a lot that you can do other than vote with your feet. If you sit back and wait them out, all you are doing is propagating the problem and leaving yourself in an unsatisfying position for longer. However, I've seen with my own eyes that organizations do take action if team members start leaving bad bosses. I've been in meetings with senior leaders who are taking notice of unusually high turnover with a particular boss. Or, they hear the complaints from people in their organization about a specific boss's leadership style, which is creating ill will. Most senior leaders abhor hearing complaints from team members, and they tend to act quickly in order to just make it go away.

The responsibility for the real effort to change the mix and have more good bosses than bad ones falls into two buckets. The first is senior leaders and the other Human Resources, assuming that this is the group in your organization tasked with helping to identify and develop excellent leaders. In most organizations, this is where the expertise resides, and it usually is placed in a prominent place in the organization so that it has a seat at the table when senior leaders make critical talent decisions.

Let's begin with the role of senior leaders, which is the more important of the two buckets. I think that the most critical job, the one that should occupy a senior leader's time, energy and thinking, more than any other activity, is making decisions about selecting, deselecting, rewarding and developing present and future leaders. I'm defining a senior leader as anyone who leads a profit center or is responsible for producing goods or services that your organization delivers to its customers, or one that drives a significant function such as Finance or Human Resources. I realize that placing so much importance on such a task may be controversial, especially when these leaders are also developing and implementing strategy, starting new businesses or product lines or developing and implementing systems changes to improve organizational performance. Perhaps a re-thinking of this task is in order. Don't look at it as a fixed pie, where leaders would spend less time on those activities that I just mentioned and more time on identifying future bosses. Instead, they should expand the pie and re-think current challenges with the identification and development of future leaders in mind. For example, let's suppose that you are developing and implementing a strategy, why not include some of the individuals that you are considering as potential future leaders in this process? Ask them what they would do if they were responsible for this new strategy. How would they handle the implementation? What do they see as the obstacles to implementation and what would they do to overcome them? By doing this, the senior leader assesses key talent and receives advice on his new strategy all at the same time.

Even in performing routine work, senior leaders can assess the ability of their subordinate bosses' potential for more significant leadership roles. When a senior leader is meeting with one of his subordinate bosses to review the status of his key initiatives, he should think about how this boss is carrying out his responsibilities. Is this person thinking and acting as someone at a senior level? How would this subordinate boss perform in my senior-level role, given the challenges? If he is thinking and acting like a boss at a higher level than he is now, then he probably has the potential to take on higher level job responsibilities.

More importantly, senior leaders, especially those in roles that can impact the organization's decision-making process for selecting future bosses, need to take a hard look at these processes (provided that they exist). It comes down to answering three critical questions. *First, do we, as an organization, have a standard and measurable definition of what a good boss is*? One of the best ways to answer this is to poll a few such leaders and ask them to describe the characteristics of a good boss; the ones that they use to make promotion decisions. A shortlist of three to five characteristics is excellent for this purpose. Hopefully there is consistency, and the characteristics being used are the right ones. If they are inconsistent or leaders need to go to Human Resources to ask what they are; then there is a problem. *Secondly, do we have processes in place to make decisions against those characteristics*? Processes practiced consistently and decisions made scientifically (and not based upon gut feel) should be the norm. *Finally, are these processes efficacious*? The idea here is that in examining the output of these processes, we see a significant supply of good bosses. This last point is crucial because I've seen organizations with world-class processes that simply aren't used by organizational leaders; instead, they rely on personal whim.

Let's look now at the role of Human Resources (HR), again assuming that this, as in most organizations, is where the responsibility for identifying and developing future bosses resides. The problem, in my experience, is that HR, tasked with this responsibility, has little power to implement it and is often viewed as not possessing the credibility to carry it out. There is a perception of weakness held by many senior leaders. This attitude is sometimes justified because many HR groups don't use the power that they have and don't effectively push senior leaders to make the right decisions.

When picking future leaders, it's easy for senior leaders to fall into the habit of picking the hard-working, loyal subordinate who is technically competent, the person that they like the most. I've seen too many HR leaders simply go along with that decision because they want to appear supportive and build a good relationship with senior leaders. This action sets up a paradox since HR ends up bringing about the very condition that they are trying to prevent. By being supportive of these decision makers with the goal of improving the relationship, HR rubber stamps decisions, causing senior leaders, in turn, to look at HR as not adding value. HR needs to understand that if they don't at least call out a wrong decision (and explain why it is a wrong decision) then they are incurring a self-inflicted wound.

If HR determines that actions are necessary to improve the talent identification process then there needs to be an honest assessment of the appetite of senior leaders for initiating the required changes. In essence, HR needs to find out if senior leaders are doing an excellent job of this currently, or they aren't doing a good job but desire to do so, or if they aren't interested in it at all. When I ask this question, very often I hear from HR that "senior leaders want to do a good job, that's why they have invested a lot of money in our leadership development programs." However I have seen many organization leaders hide behind the claim that they care about promoting good bosses because they invest so much money in leadership training, like it gives them some kind of absolution for their sins. In many cases, despite their claims, they continue to make promotion decisions without consideration of the principles of good bosses as outlined in all of that training.

The best way to honestly answer this question is to look at recently promoted bosses. What bucket would you place the majority of them in: good, bad, or ugly? Or is it equally distributed among the three of them? If you determine that senior leaders are not interested in making changes as a group, perhaps there is one senior leader who is. In my experience, when encountering an overall resistant leadership team in this area, there is often at least one leader who does want to take affirmative steps to improve leadership selection. Perhaps you could implement these steps on a much smaller scale, just for that person.

I had such a case once, where I worked with a senior leader who reported to an organization head who was not interested in making changes to a boss selection process that was ineffective. This senior leader was leading a function comprised of project teams. There was a high correlation between the success or failure of each project team and the strength of the team leader, and this senior leader was not happy with team performance overall. Not only did he see a problem with the incumbents, but he also knew the pool of future leaders was inadequate to meet the needs. I worked with him to implement a four-step process that I will outline below. As a result, he was able to make real performance improvements. We were able to identify good potential bosses for his "bench" so that he was able to swap out team leaders. The unsupportive organization head didn't care about the implementation of the process, but he did care about the tremendous bottom-line results and allowed the process to continue.

I believe that there are four steps that HR needs to take in creating and implementing a process to select good bosses. Developing this talent identification system is not an easy task because senior leaders need to buy into this process if they are going to use it to make decisions. Therefore, it is key to ensure that there is a partnership with organizational decision makers during the plan's development. As a way of beginning this process, HR should interview a good sample of mid and senior-level leaders who possess credibility. The interview should consist of HR asking the following questions:

1. Identify bosses who have failed in their jobs. What behaviors, characteristics, or attributes did they display that caused them to fail? You aren't interested in names, only the specific behaviors that caused this failure.

2. Identify the top 20% of your best performing subordinate bosses. What behaviors, characteristics, or attributes do they display that cause them to be so successful?

The objective of the exercise is to identify the characteristics of both good and bad bosses in your organization. The reason for this analysis is to prevent the "not-invented-here" syndrome that plagues many change processes. Senior leaders will be more likely to buy in to a practice if it is not just imposed from outside. The changes to the talent identification process should be modeled on global best practices, but also anchored on proven criteria of what a high performing boss is in your organization. Making this linkage is the point of the study. It is essential in this analysis to pick the right leaders, ones who are successful and will be an ally in supporting your change. When selecting the sample, it's best to err on the size of large, rather than small. Doing this not only adds credibility but also helps build buy-in since you are taking the time to talk to so many leaders who can then provide support for an upcoming change.

The second thing that HR needs in order to select good bosses is to have talent identification infrastructure based on proven scientific tools. Tools that, when combined with sound human judgment, produce the right decision. Imagine this infrastructure as a funnel. Into the wide mouth go all of those individuals who the organization believes can be future leaders. Starting with potential first-line bosses, you should place those individuals into the funnel who have displayed some leadership ability, have delivered on results, and seem to be motivated to want to lead. A similar funnel is established for second-line leaders. These are the individuals to whom the first-line bosses would report. A funnel is also developed for third-line bosses or your senior leaders. The separate funnels are needed so that you are comparing like to like. You wouldn't want to compare the leadership ability of a first-line boss to a senior leader, because the latter would have much more experience that would give him a definite advantage.

The first stop in the funnel is *on-the-job capacity*, defined as obtaining sustained superior results over time, as compared to others who were in both similar roles and confronted by similar challenges. Let's break this down and discuss it piece by piece. Anybody can have a good year. As the old saying goes, even a blind squirrel can find an occasional acorn. An individual who knows how to obtain results will deliver on them consistently over time. The comparison to others is critical since this is an excellent way to determine if this person can produce results that others who have the same experience or education have not mastered. If many similar individuals are achieving the same results, then it's not exceptional.

Basing a promotion of the achievement of results is a prevalent practice. However, I've seen two problems with it serving as the sole criterion in making talent decisions. First, there is a false assumption that past performance means future success. However, just because an individual performs well at one level does not mean that they will perform well at the next level. The challenges at the next level are very different. For example, a first level boss who does well at driving the performance of his team members gets promoted to a role that requires him to be strategic. The skill that is necessary to be successful at driving the performance of others is not the same as that required for being strategic. Secondly, not using enough rigor in the achievement of results is another problem. Specifically, I've seen times where a leader had a great year where he achieved significant results and was rewarded by a promotion to a position of greater responsibility. This leader failed in the current role because he lacked the skills or abilities to be successful. As it turned out, the achievements that won him the promotion to begin with were due to good fortune or a great team that turned in excellent results for which the boss got the credit. In sum, although results should be used, they are only a first step. Undertaking more analysis is critical before making a decision.

For those that pass through the first stop, the second stop is *long-term capacity*, which entails having faced the right challenges, possessing the motivation to want to lead, and having the right personality to want to work with others to resolve conflict and empower subordinates. Let's start by looking at what it means to face the right challenges. As we go through life, we encounter problems that we have never faced before. When we successfully overcome each challenge, we find that we have grown. In Chapter Three I described the study where I interviewed several executives about how they got to the senior level. They told me that they learned from a number of rich experiences such as taking over a part of the business that was in trouble. However, not everyone encounters or faces the same experiences and therefore, not everyone grows at the same rate as their peers who do encounter these key developmental opportunities. It's like the old saying goes: "it's not the age, but the mileage."

The motivation to want to lead is also vitally important. We should not assume that everybody who is a boss really wants the responsibility of the job. They may desire the higher pay, the big office, and the stock options, but they don't want to handle those messy people issues that bosses have to face. Good bosses, however, want to lead others. They also have the personality that is required to be successful. For example, they enjoy collaborating, which is necessary to obtain a win-win conflict resolution. They like to be around and with people, connecting with them socially as opposed to remaining aloof and distant, avoiding interaction. It can be difficult lead others effectively if you have a personality where you are naturally a loner.

For those that pass through those first two stops in the funnel, there is the third stop at the narrow neck of the funnel, which I refer to as the *capacity to be promoted*. This is the step where we determine if an individual is now ready to take on the role of greater leadership responsibility. Just because an individual has the right personality to lead and has accomplished excellent results, it doesn't mean that they are ready to take on the full-time responsibility of leading a team. For example, let's suppose that a lower level boss has demonstrated that he can handle employee problems, plan the work of others, and make the right decisions. Now he is being considered for a higher level leadership position that will require him to develop a strategy. None of his previous job responsibilities have prepared him for this particular new challenge, as we indicated earlier. Therefore, we need to test his ability to be strategic before actually placing him in the job. One of the best ways to accomplish this is to give him additional responsibility in his current role, such as developing a strategy for his team. If he does well, then he may be ready to take on that more significant role. If he doesn't do well, then we provide him some development and test him again later. Out of the narrow spout of the funnel come great leaders who have passed through all three stops.

Each of these stops should be assessed by multiple points of data, over time, using different sources. For example, when determining on-the-job capacity, your organization's performance appraisal process as well as 360-degree feedback could be used. Other sources of data, such as assessment centers, personality, and cognitive testing, could provide useful insights. The idea is that these multiple points of data should be a mix of quantitative and qualitative measures from both internal and external sources.

Having a mix of varying types of inputs reduces the chance of bias. Whatever combination of measures that the organization uses, the process should be reviewed and decisions made in an open forum with organizational leaders who possess first-hand knowledge, in a variety of settings, of these talented individuals. The more diverse the opinions that others have, the more vibrant the discussion. During these discussions, the testing data should be reviewed with the group by someone trusted as an expert in its interpretation. Validity is ensured by comparing test results to what occurred on the job. In other words, if the testing says that this individual possesses the characteristics of a micro-manager, then the group should look for on-the-job evidence that this individual does indeed micro-manage. On-the-job performance should always be the final word if there is a discrepancy between it and the testing. The assessment of these stops should never be relegated to an external testing instrument exclusively and thereby remove human judgment. Organizational leaders should have a say into who comes out of the spout of the funnel and should support their views by evidence. If their opinions aren't considered, then they won't own the outcome.

Let's take a look at an example of how the above process is used to make talent decisions. Earlier, I discussed how I worked with a senior leader to improve the quality of both incumbent bosses and his bench. I began to work with this senior leader, who, upon taking over a function, was very disappointed both with incumbent leaders and the "bench." The "bench" is defined as those who are in line for future leadership positions when they open. The team that he was leading had a track record of underperforming incumbent bosses. The so-called bench consisted of a lot of names of experienced individuals. However, there had been no testing as to whether or not these individuals could lead.

After outlining the process to this senior leader, we began to collect data on which to measure his talent pool as it passed through the funnel. For assessing *on-the-job capacity* we had the results of the organization's performance appraisal process. For the second set of data, to use for comparison, we used a 360-degree feedback process that stack ranked the survey participants from highest to lowest performer. We then surveyed the first and second-line leadership, so that we had a list of each group stacked up against their peers. For *long-term capacity*, the organization already had in place a high-potential identification process, with its own measurement tools. For the second set of data, we used a test that measured the various elements that make up leadership potential that included challenges, motivation, and personality. We put all high potentials through this process as a way to obtain a second opinion. For the *capacity to be promoted*, the organization already had a lot of assessment center data to use. For a second set of data, we decided to use the organization's succession planning process, which had been in place for years. However, this process as it stood was mostly ineffective. It was only reviewed once per year, and management didn't put much effort into it. There had been little discussion around the justification of why individuals should be successors. Therefore, we decided to conduct a review more frequently. This senior leader now expected his subordinates to justify why someone should be on the list. Successors were given "acting assignments" in the jobs that they were being considered for, as a way to see if they could perform well in that role.

The senior leader and I organized quarterly meetings to review both the status of the talent pool and the progress of assigned development actions, designed to increase individual capacity. In addition to development plan status, we reviewed the latest outputs from the six assessment checks that I underlined above, since not all were conducted at the same time. Most importantly, the senior leader held his subordinate management accountable for their part in driving the development of these future good bosses. This leader made it clear to his subordinate bosses that the amount of support that they provided and the results that they achieved would figure into his performance reviews of them.

The third step where HR needs to engage is to ensure that good bosses are selected. In my experience, this is where I see HR organizations fail consistently. They need to call out organizational leaders when they are going to make bad boss decisions. I am not suggesting that they need to fall on their swords and put their own jobs on the line. However, when leaders are going to make a bad choice, HR needs to articulate why this is the wrong decision by citing how the selected boss will behave when he starts his new job, based upon the available data. For example, the case may be that this boss will micro-manage his team and his best people will leave. Like any good doctor who tells his patient the bad news, HR needs to show the decision-making leader the x-ray. The x-ray, in this case, is the evidence that has been collected and documented that shows that this leader will micro-manage. HR also needs to provide an alternative candidate if one is available or offer assistance in making an external hire if one is not available.

I can't emphasize enough that organization leaders must own the final decision when using scientific data (such as personality or cognitive testing, or assessment data) in the decision-making process. Leaders may claim that the scientific assessment is wrong because there is evidence to the contrary, as demonstrated in the way that the candidate performs his job. As I indicated earlier, performance on the job is the final arbiter. However, even in the face of evidence from multiple points of data, I've seen organizational leaders select a boss based upon criteria that is not based upon what makes a good boss. I have heard such justifications as: "it's his turn, we like his technical ability," or "I can count on him to get things done." When speaking truth to power, citing the evidence, HR may not be listened to every time. However, when they turn out to be right about this wrong choice, which in my experience is more times than not, they will gain credibility. Conversely, if HR does nothing, credibility will be lost. The objective through this effort is to place senior leaders in a position where they realize that they are not making the right talent decisions by themselves, in the absence of data. HR has a process in place that could improve decision quality and that can be utilized when senior leaders are ready.

The fourth thing that HR should do is to educate the organization on the best-in-class talent selection systems that they are implementing. This should include not just how they work, but why the organization is taking the pains to implement them. Providing evidence to decision makers that shows how these systems will produce the desired results is critical. This evidence should come from benchmarking studies from world-class organizations that have made these changes. Supporting this evidence should be the internal research on good bosses and their relationship to superior performance done within the organization, as I described earlier. This education is vital, and it's hard to overdo it. I've known many leaders who were undereducated on the systems that their organization had put into place. For example, I've heard some of them say, "Just give me one test that does it all. I don't see why I need to spend much time on this." Leaders need to know why it is as complicated as it is and why they have to spend the time on it. HR must provide a hefty dose of exactly how this system will improve performance, beyond the fact that it is the right thing to do.

This communication has to equip these decision makers with enough understanding of how the process operates. They don't have to be experts in it—that's HR's job. However, if they don't possess at least a basic understanding of how it all works, they will discount it. It is also best to err on the side of over-communication as opposed to under-communication since this may be so new to organization decision makers, and they spend so little time on it relative to other activities. That said, one could hope to inspire a change in mindset that would lead them to consider this sort of leadership planning as one of their most essential tasks.

The best way to communicate is when organizational leaders are deciding which boss to promote. HR should weigh in on the decision with the reasons why a particular boss is the right one to be promoted and why not others, based upon the evidence as it relates to the selection system. Once there is a promotion decision, assuming it is the one that the data supports, HR should follow up with organizational leaders and highlight how this good boss is performing. They can give specific emphasis as to how his behavior is congruent with the predictions made about him based upon the data.

I realize that, for the most part, the average person who reads this chapter does not have a lot to do with the structure and systems necessary to ensure that there are good bosses in your organization. However, if you feel your organization needs to do a better job in this area, you can go to HR and ask them what they are doing about it. I've seen HR organizations that respond to this type of feedback if they hear enough of it. If you are part of HR, ask yourself whether your function is proactively ensuring that there are good bosses. Or, whether HR is taking a back seat and letting senior leaders promote the bosses that they want, even in the face of data that this individual will be a bad boss. If you are a senior leader and your organization is not performing as well as it could, what are you doing to ensure those good bosses are developed and promoted? If you are waiting for higher level leaders to tell you to do it, chances are it will never come.

Chapter Fifteen

So, You Want to Be a Better Boss?

You are currently a boss, and you want to be a better boss than you are today, which is a noble goal. Unfortunately, I have found that in most organizations, there will only be lip service from your organization to aid you in this endeavor. Over the last four decades, I have coached many leaders who wanted to be better bosses. I have conducted hundreds of leadership development programs all over the world and in a variety of organizations. I've been struck over time by the number of individuals who have said: "I know that I need to be a better boss and I know what I should do, but my boss doesn't do these things, he isn't expecting me to do it, so why should I change?" It is an argument that has some merit. As human beings, we tend to do what we are rewarded for and avoid doing things that are not. I've even known organizations that have punished those that have displayed the characteristics of a good boss. However, these are extreme cases. The most common issue is that being a good leader is not rewarded. The intention of this chapter is to aid the population of want-to-be good leaders, especially anybody in a leadership position who is not getting much, if any, support from their boss or the organization and are left on their own to develop themselves. I'm not going to spend too much time defining what a good boss is. We did a little of that earlier and there are plenty of good works out there that will help define this for you. Instead, in this chapter, I want to get into how to make this happen.

For this discussion, let's suppose that we can place the way that organizations promote bosses into three categories. *Category A* organizations make a conscious decision to promote good bosses. They have a highly robust decision-making processes that requires several points of data, usually using a scientific method. There is a standard definition of what a good boss is that senior leaders can easily articulate. No matter where you are in this organization, the process is used the same way, because senior leadership understands it, buys into and consistently applies it. This clarity of definition is supported by a performance management system that holds these leaders accountable for promoting and developing the right bosses. It doesn't mean that they are perfect in making the right decisions—even the best of talent management processes don't make the right decision 100% of the time. However, when they do make the wrong decision, *Category A* organizations step up and take action by removing a bad boss and replacing him with a good one, or at least they intend to.

Category B organizations tend to have somewhat loose systems used to try to make the right decisions about promoting good bosses. Senior management tends to place the process of selecting the right bosses as a low priority. There is little scientific data that enters into the decision-making process. The process varies widely and is used differently in different parts of the organization. In my own experience, examples of this category include such things as leaders being allowed to make "gut" decisions about selecting bosses. Or, the process of choosing bosses is something that "HR makes us do." I have even heard some senior leaders say that an organized method of selecting future bosses is a "time-consuming process that takes me away from the real work of running my organization." In other words, promoting a good boss is not considered an essential part of the job. One of the best ways to identify a *Category B* organization is to ask senior leaders what a good boss is. Unlike *Category A* organizations, the definition of a good boss is very loose and open for interpretation. Several leaders give lip-service to the "official" definition of a good boss. When it comes down to the final decision however, they will fall back on technical ability. There are also no penalties for leaders who don't use the talent selection system. In essence, the selection process lacks real discipline.

Category C organizations are those that purposely select bosses for other criteria that are not consistent with those of a good boss. The characteristics of a good boss run counter to the leadership culture. Good bosses are punished when discovered. Specifically, I've seen examples in *Category C* organizations whereby good bosses who are public about being a good boss are pulled aside and told that they need to behave more in alignment with the leadership culture if they want to have a career. In these organizations, I've also seen examples of good bosses who "fly under the radar" and avoid being discovered by organizational leaders. The good boss's stealth may sound unlikely, but it isn't that all uncommon. Let's suppose that the primary mechanism for promoting a boss is technical ability. A good boss can also be skilled technically, since being a good boss and being a technical expert aren't mutually exclusive. Since the organizational decision makers are only looking for and measuring technical ability, the good boss qualities that these individuals display may remain hidden from view unless they make a public display of them.

In *Category C* organizations, senior leaders resist an outside influence, such as that of HR, in the decision-making process for making promotion decisions. Like *Category A* organizations, senior management tends to be very clear and consistent about the types of bosses that get promoted, just that they use different criteria. Usually, the bosses that do get promoted are those that are technically competent, possess excellent educational credentials, are smart, and possess a demonstrated ability to micro-manage their subordinates. They are also adept at keeping senior leaders informed about what is going on in their respective areas of responsibility.

When describing *Category B*, I indicated an inconsistency in boss selection criteria. In some cases, this inconsistency can be so extreme that an organization can be a combination of both *Categories B and C*. Good bosses who are successful in one part of the organization can have their careers derailed when they move from the part that is *Category B* to the part that is *Category C*. This derailment can occur since their leadership style doesn't mesh with the prevailing management philosophy unless they are adept at flying under the radar. This type of combination in an organization is probably the worst of the four that I've discussed because the inconsistencies are so significant.

The best way to determine which category your organization is in is to study the behavior of bosses. Forget the organization's stated philosophy about leadership presented on the website or taught in the leadership training classes that HR offers. These don't tell you what leadership behavior the organization actually rewards. Look at the bosses who get promoted faster than others or the bosses provided with choice assignments that give them visibility. These individuals tend to be seen universally around the organization as high potentials destined for more senior-level positions. Once you have identified these bosses, the next step is to speak with trusted others who have first-hand knowledge of these individuals' strengths and weaknesses. How do these individuals lead? What qualities are they known for: is it intellect or technical ability or their personal ability to get results? Or, is it that they empower others or develop effective working relationships across organizational lines? Do they display characteristics of a good, bad, or ugly boss? Gathering multiple points of data from trusted others who have direct knowledge is critical in deciding what is genuinely the criteria used in making talent selection decisions.

Once you have accomplished your study of promotion criteria for your sample of bosses, the next step is to investigate your organization's process to conduct these promotions. You are looking for two things here. First, is the process rigorous, and second, is it followed consistently? By rigorous, I mean that it makes decisions based upon science that employ multiple points of data, as I described earlier in the chapter on what organizations need to do to ensure good bosses. During your study of the high potential bosses, you've probably already formed an opinion on how consistent your organization is in using the same criteria to make these decisions. However, one of the best sources of information on this is the group tasked with providing support to it, which could be your friendly local HR representative, or it could be a centralized function that reports to a senior leader.

Let's put all this together to help you make decisions about your career. If your analysis determines that the leaders who get promoted consistently aren't good bosses, and there is a lack of rigor in the selection processes, then you are probably residing in a *Category C* organization. In this case, it's best not to talk about your development efforts to be a good boss with more senior leaders. There is a chance that you may be working for the one-off boss who really cares about this and not just giving it lip service. However, this will be by far the exception to the rule. If you are public about your desire to be a good boss, there is a higher risk of someone in senior leadership sanctioning you by moving you lower on the succession plan until you "clean up your act." To be clear, if your desire to be a good boss outweighs your desire to remain with this organization, you should consider jumping ship and moving to an organization that is more aligned with your views of what a good boss is.

If you find that there is a mix of good and bad bosses who get promoted and a selection process that has some, but limited rigor, or inconsistently followed, then you're probably in a *Category B* organization. If being a good boss is critical for you, then you shouldn't expect much in the way of organizational support; you're on your own. If you succeed, you will get recognized by organizational leaders because you get great results and not because you are a great boss. This last point is essential because of all of the reasons that I've heard over the years explaining why an individual is not going to make an effort to be a good boss, the one that comes up the most is that it just isn't essential to the organization: "My boss, who does my performance appraisal and controls my career, doesn't care if I'm a good boss or not." The only thing that I can say is that your boss *does* care about you getting results and being a good boss increases the likelihood that you will be able to achieve excellent results. If you want a capacity-increasing development assignment that you think will benefit your career, then you probably have to lobby for it yourself. You should freely talk about your development efforts with your boss, and perhaps if you take the initiative, he may provide some support.

If your analysis leads you in the direction that some parts of the organization have loose and inconsistent practices and some parts of the organization purposely employ practices to promote the wrong bosses, then you are in *Category B/C*. What's going on is that there isn't a lot of discipline around this process at the senior level. Individual leaders are left to do what they want in their own part of the organization. Therefore, if developing your skill as a good boss is critical for you, you should spend your career in that part of the organization that is *Category B* and avoid the part of the organization that is *Category C*.

Of course, the best of all worlds is *Category A*, which is marked by a preponderance of bosses who are promoted because they are the right ones and a rigorous selection system consistently followed throughout the organization. Consider yourself very lucky because you are in the 90th percentile when it comes to quality organizations. I wish that more organizations would aspire to reach that goal. Your efforts in development should be supported and rewarded.

Once you've made the category determination and you know what constraints you will have on your development, it's now time to take some action to become a better boss. The first thing that you may want to do is to develop a list of up to three specific "good boss" behaviors that you want to build. The reason for the shortlist is that it allows you to focus. Trying to develop too many things at once is a recipe for failure. An example of a behavior that I'm referring to could be: *I want to be able to create challenging performance goals with my team members that take into account their skills, abilities, and motivations.* Each of the behaviors should possess these characteristics: they will benefit you, they will help the organization, and you are highly motivated to want to accomplish them.

The real test of a specific behavior is that you will be able to clearly see if you are making progress towards accomplishing it. In other words, there would be a way to determine "yes I'm making progress" or "no I'm not." One of the best ways to develop a skill is to take a 360-degree approach to your development. By this, I mean that you should utilize your team members, trusted peers, and (where possible) your bosses. In other words, utilize all of the people around you: 360 degrees. Using the above example, could you sit with team members some time after you set these challenging goals, and see if they are genuinely motivated to accomplish the targets that you mutually established? Before you discuss this with subordinates, could you test your plan with trusted peers who understand the organization's culture and provide you with a second opinion on its viability? You could also receive feedback from your boss, specifically on what he would see as the most challenging goals that would benefit the organization and where you could have an impact. The only caveat that I would make is that you probably shouldn't do this in *Category C* organization, since publicly saying that you want to be a good boss could get you into trouble. I've found some degree of reluctance, in the people that I've coached, in taking on the challenge of asking others to provide them with support in their development, especially from their team members. They fear that to do so would make them appear vulnerable and in need of help. Although I understand their concerns, I believe that they are missing an important point: good bosses engage in life-long learning and they encourage others to do the same. What better way to do this than to set a good example by asking others to support you in your development?

As you are rolling out your new behaviors, the feedback from others over time could tell you if you are successful, since effectively changing some of your behavior to become a good boss could take years. You could, on occasion, send an email to these trusted others, with your shortlist of behaviors and ask them: am I getting better? Am I getting worse, or am I not changing? Ask them to think it over, and suggest getting together to talk about it. Along the same lines as getting feedback from trusted others, you could also use the services of a coach. Of course, trained professional coaches would be of value. However, a coach doesn't have to be an expert. A wise role model who possesses the behaviors that you are seeking to develop could work just as well. Sticking with the above example, you could consult with a peer who is good at working with team members to set goals.

Another powerful way to develop is through the power of reflection. I wish that I'd used this tool earlier in my career as a way to determine how to deal with my bad or ugly bosses. When I did start using it, I was able to develop many of the techniques that I've described in this book. What has worked for me is that I dedicated time to this task. When trying to improve the working relationship with an ugly boss, I made a point that every Friday, when I got in my car to go home after a long work week, to ask myself three fundamental questions. First, what is working with the relationship with this boss that I want to continue? Secondly, what is not working with the relationship with this boss that I want to do less of or stop altogether? Finally, what new actions can I take that I'm not currently doing that could generate more improvement?

As you can see, this exercise is not very difficult. The real challenges are taking the time to do it, being honest with yourself about what's not working, and focusing on what is. Setting up the dedicated time of every Friday after work was something to which I could commit. As far as honesty is concerned, it is natural that we tend to not be tough on ourselves when it comes to something that we need to change. After all, think of the bad habits that you've unsuccessfully tried to change over the years.

This chapter focused on ways that bosses could become good bosses. However, the methods that I outlined for development could equally apply if you aren't a boss and don't want to become one. I've used these methods with equal success in roles when I was a boss as when I was an individual contributor. The key is to focus on something important to you, involve others in your development, and often reflect to ensure progress.

Chapter Sixteen

It's Up to You

Forbes magazine reported on the results of a global study conducted by the University of Manchester's Business School on how toxic bosses affect team members. Their description of a toxic boss equates to what I have described as a bad boss. The study reported lower job satisfaction and productivity as a result of these toxic bosses, the effects of which spilled over into employees' personal lives even to the point of causing clinical depression.[vi] In another article, the Washington Post reported on several global research projects that asserted that bad bosses were making their team members physically sick. These studies also found that team members who reported to good bosses had a lower risk of heart disease and other physical ailments than those that reported to bad bosses.[vii] I have been looking at studies like this for at least the last 20 years. Most of these studies conclude by presenting some excellent solutions, much as they did 20 years ago. However, little changes in our work lives as we continue to experience an over-supply of bad bosses.

I became aware of one of these studies by listening to a morning radio talk show. After informing the listening audience about the research, the two hosts joked about the fact that everybody hates their boss. Of course, that remark was hyperbole. However, the sentiment behind it was not. Most of us who work for a bad boss simply have to "suck it up" and live with it. Or at least, if you had that belief before, I hope that as a result of reading this book you don't any longer.

There is an old workplace adage that says *you need to take control of your career*. I have heard this mentioned in many types of organizations all over the world, but never in the context of the subject matter of this book. However, in the case of improving the ability to work with your boss or to find a good one to work for, it is particularly true. As I think back over my career, I turned in my best performance working for the good bosses. They encouraged me to stretch my skills and abilities, captured my motivation, offered encouragement, and helped me to develop my capacity to produce even better results. For the bad bosses that I worked for, my performance was at best mediocre. They placed me in situations where I used a fraction of my skills, provided little direction, and kept me in the dark about expectations or concerns that I should have known about. They then blind-sided me when those enigmatic expectations were not achieved. When I looked at my output versus my capacity to deliver exceptional results, over time I produced much more for the good bosses, yet I was the same person for both the good and bad bosses. I possessed the same skills, abilities, and motivations. I had the same desire to do great work and the same caring about the success of the organization that paid my salary.

When assessing my sense of job satisfaction, there was no comparison between the types of bosses. With good bosses, I looked forward to coming to work every day. With bad bosses, I dreaded it and felt exhausted and frustrated when I went home at night. What is fascinating is that in many cases, I was doing the same type of work for both bosses. About 80% of the time, I gained real satisfaction from what I was doing. It was the quality of the boss that, when added to the equation, changed that percentage up or down. The good bosses created an environment where I felt proud of the work that I did. I felt good about myself, which in turn translated into positive interactions with my friends and family. The bad bosses gave me sleepless nights over trying to figure out how to deal with seemingly unsolvable problems, or in other cases, trying to understand what I was supposed to do to succeed with these people. I questioned my abilities, not because I was challenged to do things that I've never done before, but because I was confronted with problems or situations that I couldn't impact and because I didn't understand my boss's expectations. My requests for clarification were often rebuked with "I don't have time for this right now" or "You need to figure this out yourself."

I've spent much of my career coaching others. I wish that I had a nickel for every time that someone would come to me and want to talk about their bad boss and havoc he created in their life. Besides not having the nickels, I spent a small fortune on tissues. What was readily apparent in those discussions with the aggrieved team member was that they were spending time and energy agonizing over what this relationship was doing to their lives at work and at home, energy that could have been spent on making them more productive. In some cases, this relationship was causing burgeoning health issues that could mean reduced productivity in the future, just as was reported in the above research projects. In some of these sessions, we were able to talk through how to work with the boss. However, there were many occasions where it was clear that it was hopeless. In too many of these situations, I found that the person I was coaching offered all types of coping excuses like "maybe he'll get fired or promoted soon," or "perhaps he will change as he gets more comfortable or experienced with the job." These individuals were afraid to do what they knew that they needed to do. They decided to live with the pain rather than to address the issue. For some, it was a lack of confidence, and with others, it was that they didn't know how to deal with it. For some, it was both.

Knowing what action to take and when is a complicated process. You can err by not taking action, acting too soon, or not fully understanding the situation. I've made all three of these mistakes. One time I changed jobs, leaving a bad boss to work for a good one that was offering me some fascinating work. Six weeks after I made the transition, my bad boss got a promotion, and his replacement was an ugly one. I have also stayed with bad bosses too long, rationalizing that it will get better someday. Eventually I found that there was no improvement; it just got worse. I have also misdiagnosed bosses before and applied the wrong remedy, because of my tendency of being impatient. To prevent being too quick in acting, make sure that you collect multiple points of data on this boss. Ask yourself, honestly, why you need to take action to leave. Is it because he is a bad boss, or is it that he reminds you of the brother-in-law that you don't like? Don't rely merely on your own view. Seek the counsel of trusted others who have an accurate picture of the person. Do they share the same assessment that you do? Have they seen and can they articulate several specific examples of the same behavior that you find troubling? This last point is critical since I've seen several times where bosses act one way towards one team member and another way entirely towards another. Knowing this can be significant since it could mean the difference between a bad boss or an ugly one. I've been in situations before where I was having difficulty with a boss, and other members were not. By understanding what they were doing to maintain a positive working relationship, I was able to make adjustments.

I made the point earlier in this book that it is essential to look for a good boss to work for early in your career, as this boss will help you to identify your strengths, weaknesses, and motivations. Your skills will grow exponentially more in a shorter period than they will working for an ugly boss. I contend, based upon my study of successful leaders, that there is a direct relationship between those who had successful careers and those that had a great boss early on in that career. However, it's not just early in your career that a good boss is beneficial. I've worked for good bosses all through my career, and I grew at every opportunity. Typically, we tend to focus on the quality of the work when making a job change. I suggest that the quality of the boss should be most important. Remember, a good boss can help you turn an average job into a great one.

Most of the bosses that you will work for will be ugly ones. If you want to work with that boss, you will need to be proactive, understand them, and then develop a trusting, win-win working relationship. If you take short cuts and just look out for yourself, you probably won't be successful. Look for ways for both of you to succeed together. You can only win when that ugly boss achieves his goals, and it's up to you to help him to do that.

If you are a senior leader and make decisions on who the future bosses are, do you promote and reward bosses based upon the behaviors displayed by the good bosses that we've discussed? Or, do you select based upon their technical ability, educational credentials, or some other behaviors that are not consistent with those of good bosses? Do you take an active part in the development of future bosses by ensuring that they have the right on-the-job assignments that will develop them? Or, do you simply allow them to take leadership development courses, as the primary method of development? Finally, if you don't foster the right environment for good bosses to rise in your organization, does your organization need to improve its performance? If it does, then you need to reorder your priorities to ensure that you are pacing your time and energy in this effort.

If you are an HR leader, responsible for the organizational processes for selecting and developing future leaders, are you educating leaders on what good bosses are and the impact that they will have on performance? Do you maintain an efficacious boss selection process and defend its outputs in the face of resistance from senior leaders? Or, do you stand by while senior leaders make the wrong decisions about choosing future bosses?

While reading this book, you've probably thought, at times, that you are doing your boss's job for him by implementing some of the solutions that I've discussed. What I have suggested does take time, energy, and risk. However, if you place those things on one side of the balance sheet and compare it to the possible gain, you'll see the payoff. That potential gain comes in terms of reduced frustration, higher job satisfaction, and an increased chance of career success. There is another price to pay when working with a bad or ugly boss whose effective leadership is causing performance problems, and that is that it could impede your own career success. Pull out your resume and highlight your accomplishments in one color for the time that you worked for a bad boss and highlight in another color those accomplishments when you worked for a good boss. I suggest that, in most cases, there is a marked difference. Now, imagine you are interviewed by a job recruiter and having to justify the dearth of accomplishments on your resume for the period working for your bad boss.

When you have been dealt a bad hand in the form of a bad or ugly boss, you can either passively submit or take action. You can (and should) choose to leave your bad boss and hunt for a good one, or take affirmative action to improve the relationship with your ugly boss. What happens next is up to you.

Endnotes

[i] Sorenson, Susan, (2013, June 20) *How Employee Engagement Drives Growth,*

http://www.gallup.com/businessjournal/163130/employee-engagement-drives-growth.
[ii] Beck, Randall and Harter, Jim (2015, April 21) *Managers Account for 70% of Variance in Employee Engagement,* http://www.gallup.com/businessjournal/182792/managers-account-variance-employee-engagement.aspx
[iii] McGregor, Douglas The Human side of Enterprise, McGraw Hill Education, republished 2006
[iv] Gilbert, G.M. Nuremberg Diary, First Da Capo Press republished 1995
[v] Pierre Gurdjian, Thomas Halbeisen, and Kevin Lane (2014, January) https://www.mckinsey.com/featured-insights/leadership/why-leadership-development-programs-fail
[vi] Moran, Amy, (2017, January 15) *Study Reveals How Damaging A Toxic Boss Can Really Be* https://www.forbes.com/sites/amymorin/2017/01/15/study-reveals-how-damaging-a-toxic-boss-really-can-be/#18e31cf62497
[vii] Shannonhouse, Rebecca (2014, October 20) *Is Boss Making You Sick?* *https://www.washingtonpost.com/national/health-science/is-your-boss-making-you-sick/2014/10/20/60cd5d44-2953-11e4-8593-da634b334390_story.html*

www.ingramcontent.com/pod-product-compliance
Lightning Source LLC
Chambersburg PA
CBHW030632220526
45463CB00004B/1499